THE REALM OF RHETORIC

The Realm of Rhetoric

CH. PERELMAN

Translated by William Kluback

Introduction by Carroll C. Arnold

UNIVERSITY OF NOTRE DAME PRESS

NOTRE DAME   LONDON

Originally published as
L'Empire rhétorique:
rhétorique et argumentation

Library of Congress Cataloging in Publication Data

Perelman, Chaïm.
The realm of rhetoric.

Translation of: L'empire rhétorique.
Bibliography: p.
Includes index.
1. Reasoning. 2. Rhetoric. I. Title.
BC177.P38413   808   79-66378
ISBN 0-268-01604-6   AACR2
ISBN 0-268-01605-4 (pbk.)

Manufactured in the United States of America

Contents

Introduction

THE REALM OF RHETORIC is an English translation of Professor Perelman's *L'Empire rhétorique: rhétorique et argumentation,* published at Paris in 1977. The book develops and adds to analyses of argumentation originally presented by Perelman and Mme. L. Olbrechts-Tyteca in their *The New Rhetoric: A Treatise on Argumentation,* published in French in 1958 and in English in 1969. I am honored to have been asked to introduce this new work to American readers.

Professor Perelman's account of how his interest in the nature of argument and rhetoric arose helps one to understand his work. As a student of philosophy and law, Perelman undertook to study the nature of justice. He soon faced a question which popular systems of philosophy and logic failed to answer satisfactorily. The question was: By what processes do we *reason* about values? The question was inevitable because one cannot arrive at clear conclusions concerning how justice or any other value is distinguished from its opposite without understanding how "cases" are made for and against that value. Finding no adequate expositions of these argumentative processes in existing philosophical literature, Perelman and Mme. Olbrechts-Tyteca undertook a detailed study of "texts which attempt to have a value or a rule prevail, showing that such an action or choice is preferable." They analyzed "writing of moralists and politicians, speakers extolling this or that behavior, leading newspaper articles, all kinds of justifications."[1] Their basic question can be expressed as: What does justification of values "look like" in actual, verbal discourse? *The Realm of Rhetoric* presents their major findings in concise form, together with additional observations developed by Perelman in the years since his original investigation.

Perelman's independent study of what people actually do when they argue about values reconfirmed the ancients' contention that when one's initial premises or instances or assumptions are disputable, the best possible argument can only follow "a method by which we shall be able to reason from generally accepted opinions about any problem . . . and shall ourselves, when sustaining an argument, avoid saying anything self-contradictory."[2] As Perelman points out, the modern aspiration to arrive at *certain* conclusions in philosophy through general arguments is traceable to such figures as Rudolf Agricola and Peter Ramus in the history of rhetoric and René Descartes and Baruch Spinoza in the history of philosophy. But the arguments which Perelman studied showed clearly that to equate the principles and processes of practical argument with principles and processes of formal logic and mathematics is mistaken, as Aristotle originally asserted.

In contemporary American treatises on rhetoric and argument this equating of the processes of formal logic with those of general argument is gradually disappearing, but there still remains an ambivalence to which Perelman would object.[3] Perelman contends for a completely different kind of analysis. He is disturbed that the claims to rationality made by philosophers do not lead to agreement, so he inspects what philosophers and others actually do in arguing. He seeks to identify, in their verbal structures, how arguers claim *rationality*. He does not make purely linguistic, semiotic, or psychological analyses of verbal forms.

Rather, without denying the usefulness of these kinds of analysis, Perelman concentrates on: How do claims to reasonableness arise in prose that is not formally logical? What does "reasonable" mean for someone who speaks of "reasonable men" or "beyond reasonable doubt"? Raising such questions has led him to notice many ways of arguing in addition to the quasi-logical methods—the methods conventionally discussed by writers of American textbooks.

Perelman was led to observe that the acceptability of assumptions about the nature of reality gives some arguments their qualities of rationality; that arguments from example, illustration, and model do not really pretend to be inductions but appear rational by virtue of the "rules" they imply; that metaphors can argue as surely as extended analogies; that dissociating certain notions from primary conceptions can render the primary conceptions reasonable; that presumed relations between persons and their actions allow rational conclusions; and that amplifying and ordering ideas and arguments serve not only as dispositional and stylistic actions but can strengthen or weaken the reasonableness of claims. Not all of these observations about the sources of rationality in our arguments are new, nor does Perelman claim so (Aristotle and Roman rhetoricians noted several). What is new in Perelman's analysis in his notice that claims to rationality are embedded in a number of verbal structures that have heretofore been treated as either exclusively ornamental or dispositional. He has also enlarged our understanding of argument by noting numerous subforms of argumentation within each of the general types he identifies.

Another unconventional feature of Perelman's analysis is that he abandons traditional distinctions between rhetoric and dialectic. Like certain other contemporary scholars,[4] Perelman finds Aristotle's attempt to maintain this distinction irregular and functionally unnecessary. Perelman contends that in both dialectic and rhetoric, as traditionally defined, "it is in terms of an audience that argumentation develops." Therefore, how "opinionable" ideas must be argued will be substantially the same in either circumstance because the arguer is always seeking the adherence of some *other* person or persons to an undemonstrable thesis.[5] So the "realm of rhetoric" that Perelman discusses in this book is the entire universe of argumentative discourse. He seeks to discover the basic methods that are used in contingent arguments addressed to audiences of any sort.

The major claims Perelman makes in this book about such arguing can be summarized as follows.

1. Argumentation proceeds *in*formally, not according to the forms and rules of formal deduction and induction.

2. Arguments are always *addressed to audiences* (possibly the arguer's self) for the purpose of inducing or increasing those audiences' adherence to the theses presented.

3. To achieve any degree of success with their audiences, arguments have to proceed from premises that are *acceptable* to the audiences. The arguer may or may not include himself or herself among the audiences that are immediately addressed.

4. The arguing always includes procedures by which ideas and values can be given special *presence* (in the French sense of being *made* present) in the minds of those addressed.

5. Ambiguity is never entirely avoidable in arguments because the language which must be used is inevitably equivocal in some degree and because the terms that are available are often open to more than a single interpretation.

6. The relationships (liaisons) of concepts and attitudes are created and dissolved by verbal techniques which are distinguishable from one another. The major types of these techniques are:

a. Quasi-logical arguments which claim to be rational because they resemble the patterns of formal reasoning.

b. Arguments that are based on claims concerning the structure of reality (e.g., that phenomena succeed one another, that causes always produce effects).

c. Arguments based on examples, illustrations, and models, all of which imply and allegedly represent the operation of overriding rules or laws or principles.

d. Clarifications of one idea *(theme)* by associating it with another *(phoros),* as in analogy or metaphor.

e. Processes by which some feature(s) of an idea is detached or dissociated from it so that the primary idea can be seen as without objectionable or incompatible features.

f. Amplification or abridgment of ideas or values.

g. Imposing special orders on ideas or arguments.

Chapters 2 through 13 of *The Realm of Rhetoric* amplify and illustrate these major ways of giving rational justification to our claims in argument. Of course, many subforms of these patterns are also identified and discussed.

Perelman claims that all argumentation of the sorts just outlined is *rhetorical* rather than "logical" or "valid" in the sense we usually assign to those terms. What this distinction means can be seen if we consider some of the major conditions under which all general argumentation takes place.

First, most of the claims we make in arguing are not self-evidently true; they must be *made* to seem reasonable. They cannot be "proved" completely; they must be *judged to be reasonable* by those to whom the claims and their supports are presented. But this means that what the audience knows or thinks it knows must be brought into support of or at least rendered consonant with the claim being made. What is said in arguing *and* what the audience knows and feels must, together, seem reasonable. Moreover, since the claims we argue for cannot be demonstrated to be totally and finally true, we cannot hope that the adherence we win for a claim will be total and irrevocable. There will always be room for doubt and for a change of view. What one can sensibly seek, then, is a *degree* of acceptance of a claim.

In discussing this aspect of every arguer's *rhetorical* situation Perelman makes a happy choice of terms. Instead of writing of "acceptance" and "rejection" of claims, he speaks of the arguer as seeking "to elicit or increase the adherence of an audience" [*"provoquer ou accroître l'adhésion d'un auditoire"*]. The term *adherence* reminds us better than such terms as "agree-disagree," "accept-reject," or "approve-disapprove" that a choice rather than an irrevocable position is all we can hope for in arguing. We can only engage with someone else or with ourselves for the purpose of eliciting degrees of adherence or allegiance to ideas. This is exercise of rhetoric, not of formal proof, and it is the nature of all argumentation.

Implicit in what we have just said is a second, crucial condition of all argument. Since we argue for people and not machines, we must recognize that an audience's choices and judgments are affected not only by their knowledge and experience but by their situations at the time of confronting our arguments. Thus methods of arguing must shift as the nature and conditions of the audience shift. Argument that is addressed to a particular audience (oneself at a particular moment or a specific group of others at a particular time or place) cannot be the same as argument addressed to another particular audience, and argument addressed to all reasonable persons or to all experts in a given field must differ from arguments we would address to particular audiences. These variable conditions, which alter the possibilities of argument, are recognized by Professor Perelman throughout *The Realm of Rhetoric*.

A third, constraining condition of all argument that is recognized in the outline above is the ambiguity of the language we must use. The relationships between linguistic terms and the concepts or images they symbolize are never entirely stable. In mathematics or formal logic, terms and signs such as *x* or *p* and *:* or *::* can have firm, fixed meanings by arbitrary agreement, but this is not true of the terms that are used in discussing disputable matters. As Perelman points out, every definition implicitly admits that some other definition is possible; otherwise, there would be no need to define in the first place. Likewise, every evaluative term or statement implicitly admits that one *could* give a different evaluation and make some defense of it. Were it not so, we would have no need to express *our* evaluation. So a credible defense of a thesis must not only express the claim and give it support that is credible to the audience, but the argument must also justify the claimant's terminology and choices in building up relationships. How is this done?

In Perelman's language, an arguer must find methods by which to give his terms, his ideas, and the relationships he asserts *presence.* In chapter 4 Perelman equates giving *presence* with *emphasizing,* with actively bringing thoughts and methods prominently before the minds of the audience addressed. In the language of Gestalt psychology, we might say that each claim and its rationality must be made a "figure." Indeed, the special resources for giving thoughts and methods *presence* are resources which traditional rhetoric tends to identify as "figures" of thought and language. Perelman identifies a number of them in chapter 4 and discusses their potentialities for highlighting—giving *presence* to—ideas and methods of arguing.

To summarize this third point that Perelman makes concerning argumentation, we can say that since language always introduces degrees of equivocality and ambiguity into our communication, our arguing must not only reveal the credibility of our claims but must also contend, by a variety of rhetorical techniques, for the significance, the deserved *presence,* of the claims and the methods of their support. Once more, the task is rhetorical rather than purely logical, for in formal logic or mathematics these strategies of emphasizing would be out of place. In argument they are essential.

Fourth, we should notice the special ways in which ideas become connected, according to the outline above. Again, Perelman's choice of terms is happy. He speaks of arguers as establishing *liaisons* among ideas (see chap. 6, pp. 00-00, and later discussions). *Liaison* admirably expresses what one can and cannot establish concerning the relationships among data and/or arguments. A liaison is a contact, possibly an intimacy, maintained between persons or groups in order to ensure some concerted action or achievement. In French, Perelman's primary language, the term further connotes a joining, a conjunction, a connection, an acquaintance. In cookery, "liaison" means a "thickening" achieved in, say, a sauce or a soup by adding such a substance as eggs or cream.

All of these nuances are right for expressing the degree to which ideas can be integrated in argumentative discourse. Ideas cannot be permanently locked together or irrevocably related where what is known or believed is only probably so. But ideas can be placed in "contact" with one another, made "intimates," "thickened" together. These are the strongest bonds we can build when we argue about matters that are not open to final, absolute proof. When he uses the term *liaison,* Perelman is urging us to notice the contrast between rhetoric and formal logic, where relationships are claimed for ideas. In formal logic or mathematics, a term or concept or proposition can formally *entail*—involve by necessity— other terms or concepts or propositions. But Perelman emphasizes with special clarity that such entailments are never possible in argument; it is the rhetorical nature of argumentation that only liaisons among terms and notions can be built.

Noting the several limitations under which argumentation always occurs, according to Perelman, brings us to the main grounds on which theories of argument such as Perelman's are challenged. Bluntly put, the basic charge is that if argumentation can only be as Perelman describes it, there can be no "valid" way of distinguishing a "good" argument from a "bad" one, in which case nothing really useful can be accomplished through argument. A moralist might put the question thus: "Is there *no* establishment of 'right' and 'wrong' through argument?" Some logicians assert: "If only liaisons can be established by arguments, there can be no 'true' rationality, and in that case argumentation is a process scarcely worth serious study." As Professor Perelman points out, this is, in fact, what philosophers who are committed to logical positivism have insisted. A sociologist might ask: "Is the social life of mankind then to be conceived as an endless round of claimings and counterclaimings, with no resolutions of disagreements except by applying force and legal decision making?" And general philosophers are apt to ask: "Does nothing distinguish 'rigorous' philosophical argument from the 'loose' arguing we see in politics, advertising, religion, or private affairs?" These are questions and charges that have been leveled against the conception of argument presented in *The Realm of Rhetoric,* though the general view presented in this book has support from a number of twentieth-century rhetoricians and philosophers, including some philosophers of science.

To such queries and charges those who share Perelman's understanding of rhetorical argument respond in what at first seems a paradoxical way. They grant that all arguments, including their own, are inconclusive, but they insist that their arguments are "convincing." Perelman's response is clear:

> All intellectual activity which is placed between the necessary and the arbitrary is reasonable to the degree that it is maintained by arguments and eventually clarified by controversies which normally do not lead to unanimity [chap. 14, p. 000].

Perelman grants, then, that his analysis of the procedures and the role of argument as rhetoric is itself arguable. *The Realm of Rhetoric* is not intended to end discussion of what argument can and cannot be or of what settlements arguments can or ought to produce. Perelman aims at making a "convincing" case that argumentation settles matters only when the audiences to which it is addressed arrive at some consensus on the issue argued.

On this view, controversy over the nature of rhetorical discourse, and its services to us, must continue (clarifying, one hopes, mooted issues and claims) until a significant set of audiences understandingly adheres to Perelman's or some other interpretation of what it is to argue with self and others. We, as readers, are invited to weigh and argue the claims and liaisons of ideas which Professor Perelman puts forth. He is seeking to elicit or increase our adherence to his theses. His methods are, by his own definitions, rhetorical, and we should take notice of what sort of audience he takes us to be. He addresses us as an informed, philosophically inclined audience, inviting us to participate with him in a centuries-old argument over the "true" nature of what seems a behavior natural to our kind: argumentation.

Because Professor Perelman addresses us as a philosophically inclined audience, it may be useful to American readers to conclude this introduction with two historical notes.

As Perelman indicates in his first chapter, there has been in Western culture a long-held supposition that theories of verbal expression and theories of philosophical inquiry can and ought to exist apart. This notion has been at the root of the historic "conflict" between philosophers and rhetoricians, a conflict which in rather recent years has come under serious challenge.[6] Among the consequences of this conflict have been confinement of rhetorical scholarship to studies of verbal style, especially the "figures" to which Perelman often refers, and very little consideration of philosophical aspects of communicative, verbal discourse. This separation of thought about style and thought about philosophy has marked European thinking severely until the present century. Questions concerning the rhetorical aspects of philosophical thought have been extensively discussed in Europe only in the last quarter century. Professor Perelman's writing reflects the newness of these considerations in European (and British) intellectual life.

Americans, however, draw on a slightly different and somewhat longer tradition of thinking about rhetorical communication, though their tradition has not until recently become philosophical. A broad conception of rhetoric, somewhat like that which Perelman urges, began to emerge in the United States in the second decade of this century. It did not, however, arise from the interests of philosophers but from the interests of students of prose composition. Charles Sears Baldwin's essay, "Rhetoric," in Monroe's *Cyclopaedia* (1914) early and influentially insisted that rhetorical behavior involves more than stylistic manipulations. Baldwin urged recovery of the full dimensions of rhetoric by re-exploring classical theories of composition, an enterprise he greatly furthered by publishing his *Ancient Rhetoric and Poetic* (1924) and *Medieval Rhetoric and Poetic* (1928). During the same period and later, a group of classical, rhetorical, and literary scholars, sometimes referred to as the Cornell University School, was advancing historical and critical study of rhetorical theory and practice. Lane Cooper, Everett Lee Hunt, Hoyt H. Hudson, Herbert A. Wichelns, Wilbur Samuel Howell, Harry Caplan, and a number of others carried out and directed a wide variety of studies, all tending to establish in American thinking the classical contention that rhetorical activity is conceptual as well as stylistic. Meanwhile, from its founding in 1914, the Speech Communication Association and its affiliates in the United States stressed the importance of rhetorical studies of all sorts, significantly including psychological investigations. Two especially influential figures applied then-contemporary psychological theories in developing explanations of rhetorical behavior: James A. Winans, furnishing a Jamesian, pragmatic interpretation, and Charles H. Woolbert, providing a Watsonian behavioristic account. Influences of their early and exceedingly different lines of inquiry into the nature of rhetoric remain strong.

The American tradition in rhetorical studies has until recently been more heavily historical, psychological, and critical than philosophical, but the premise that rhetorical behavior is first conceptual and secondarily linguistic was well established in this country by the time of the Second World War. Some American readers of *The Realm of Rhetoric,* who have inherited the tradition just described, may be perplexed by Professor Perelman's vigorous defense of a kind of study that has been pursued in this country for some seventy years. They will need to remind themselves that the legitimacy of rhetorical studies that are not exclusively linguistic has been granted in Europe by only the present generation of scholars.

When Perelman says that "not long ago rhetoric was disdained in Europe and even in the United States" (chap. 14, p. 000), he is quite right; however, American readers who are under forty are unlikely to remember the disdain with which pioneering rhetorical scholars were met in this country two generations ago.

Readers who inherit the American historical-psychological-critical tradition in rhetoric may also need to take special note that Professor Perelman writes as a philosopher. He is therefore specially concerned to say what distinguishes philosophical argumentation from other rhetoric—a matter of limited concern among Americans until the last twenty years. Perelman's answer is unique and has been argued by philosophers for almost thirty years.[7] As phrased in the present book, philosophical argument is argument "addressed to everyone, to a universal audience composed of those who are disposed to hear him, and are capable of following his argumentation" (chap. 2, p. 00). Philosophers have not reached consensus concerning the adequacy and utility of this definition of philosophical argument, but Perelman's concept of "the universal audience" is important and original with him. It deserves each reader's thoughtful consideration, for it implies that the quality of argumentation is to be judged by the intellectual qualifications and expertise of the audience which is willing to take the argument seriously and, perhaps, adhere to it in some degree. For more than a quarter century Perelman has contended that makers of arguments may choose to address either particular audiences or all reasonable persons, known and unknown, who are expert in the subject argued about and competent to judge the methods used in argument. To choose the second kind of audience is the highest and most demanding choice open to arguers, Perelman thinks, and when one so argues, he or she argues philosophically. As we have seen, Perelman denies that even this kind of argument can have formal, logical "validity"; its merits, like the merits of any other argument, can be judged only by the wisdom of those who do or could take it seriously and adhere to it in some degree.

When he takes this stand, Perelman faces forthrightly the most serious and mooted question in theory of argument today: What gives an argument "worth" or "validity" if we grant that the supports of argumentation can never establish conclusions as *necessarily* true? Perelman says, in effect, that our arguments are as worthy as our efforts to encourage reasonable people to follow the "rule of justice"—to treat similar matters, things, and persons similarly. His answer has roused much interest, but there are those who have challenged it. We who read Professor Perelman's new book are invited to participate in an ongoing debate over whether this test of the "worth" of arguments is as firm a test as we can have.

CARROLL C. ARNOLD
Professor Emeritus, Speech Communication
The Pennsylvania State University
University Park, Pennsylvania

1. *Logic, Dialectic, Philosophy, and Rhetoric*

IN HIS REMARKS on ancient rhetoric, Roland Barthes correctly observed that "rhetoric must always be read in its structural interplay with its neighbors—grammar, logic, poetics, and philosophy."[1] I would add that in order best to define and situate rhetoric, we must also clarify its relationship to dialectic.

Aristotle in his *Organon* distinguished two types of reasoning—analytic and dialectic. He undertook a study of the former in the *Prior and Posterior Analytics*, and this study can be considered in the history of philosophy as the basis of formal logic. However, modern logicians have failed to see that Aristotle studied dialectical reasoning in the *Topics*, the *Rhetoric*, and the *Sophistical Refutations*. This failure is caused by their inability to see the importance of the latter works, which made Aristotle not only the father of formal logic but also the father of the theory of argumentation.

In his *Analytics*, Aristotle studied the forms of valid inference and specifically the syllogism which allows us, certain hypotheses being given, to infer from them a necessary conclusion. If *A* is *B* and if *B* is *C*, the necessary result is that *A* is *C*. The inference is valid whether the premises are true or false, but the conclusion is true only if the premises are true. This inference is characterized both by the fact that it is purely formal, that is, valid whatever be the contents of the terms *A, B,* and *C* (the only condition being that each letter be replaced by the same value each time it is used), and at the same time by the fact that it establishes a connection between the truth of the premises and that of the conclusion. Since truth is a property of the proposition and is independent of personal opinion, analytical reasoning is demonstrative and impersonal. But this is not the case with dialectical reasoning. Aristotle tells us that dialectical reasoning presupposes premises which are constituted by generally accepted opinions.[2] The generally accepted premises are those "which are accepted by everyone or by the majority or by the philosophers—i.e., by all, or by the majority, or by the most notable and illustrious of them."[3]

In certain cases, what is generally acceptable is probable, but this probability cannot be confounded with calculable probability. On the contrary, the meaning of the word *eulogos,* which is usually translated as "generally acceptable" or "acceptable," has a qualitative aspect which brings it closer to the term "reasonable" than to the term "probable." We should note that probability concerns only past or future facts or events, while the theses which are under discussion can deal with nontemporal questions such as "Is the world finite or infinite?" or "Is democracy the best form of government?"

We can immediately see that dialectical reasoning begins from theses that are generally accepted, with the purpose of gaining the acceptance of other theses which could be or are controversial. Thus it aims either to persuade or convince. But instances of dialectical reasoning are not made up of series of valid and compelling inferences; rather, they advance *arguments* which are more or less strong, more or less convincing, and which are never purely formal. Moreover, as Aristotle noted,[4] a persuasive argument is one that persuades the person to whom it is addressed; this means that, unlike the processes of analytical reasoning, a dialectical argument can not be impersonal, for it derives its value from its action upon the mind of some person. As a consequence, it is necessary that we clearly distinguish analytical from dialectical reasoning, the former dealing with truth and the latter with justifiable opinion. Each field of thought requires a different type of discourse; it is as inappropriate to be satisfied with merely reasonable arguments from a mathematician as it would be to require scientific proofs from an orator.[5]

Now, it is in relation to this distinction that we can see how the innovation introduced by Peter Ramus turned out to be an error that was fatal for rhetoric. Beginning with the trivium, with the arts of discourse, Ramus defined grammar as the art of speaking well, that is, of speaking correctly; dialectic as the art of reasoning well; and rhetoric as the art of the eloquent and ornate use of language.[6] Taking dialectic to be the "general art of inventing and judging all things,"[7] he asserted that "there is only one method, which is that of Plato and Aristotle, . . . this method is found in Virgil and Cicero, in Homer and Demosthenes, it presides over mathematics, philosophy, opinions, and human conduct."[8]

Thus with a flourish Ramus tossed aside the Aristotelian distinction between analytical and dialectical judgments, justifying his attitude in this way: "for although some cognitive things are necessary and scientific while others are contingent and subject to opinion, if in every case the action of seeing is common to seeing immutable as well as mutable colors, so the art of knowing, i.e., dialectic and logic, is one and the same doctrine for the apperception of all things."[9]

The scope that was now given to dialectic, as embracing both the study of valid inferences and the art of finding and discovering arguments, deprived Aristotle's rhetoric of its two essential elements, invention and disposition, leaving only elocution, the study of ornate forms of language. It is in

this spirit that Ramus' friend, Omer Talon, published in
Cologne in 1572 the first systematic rhetoric limited to the
study of figures. According to Talon, the figure is "a
garnishing of speech, wherein the course of the same is
changed from the more simple and plain manner of
speaking."[10] In this way classical rhetoric came into being—
this rhetoric of figures which led progressively from the
degeneration to the death of rhetoric.

It is certainly well known that modern logic, developed
since the middle of the nineteenth century under the
influence of Kant and the mathematical logicians, identifies
logic not with dialectic but with formal logic, with Aristotle's analytical reasoning, and completely neglects dialectical reasoning as foreign to logic. In this, modern logic
commits an error similar to that of Ramus. If it is undeniable
that formal logic is a separate discipline which lends itself,
like mathematics, to operation and calculation, it is also
undeniable that we reason even when we do not calculate—
in private deliberation or public discussion, in giving
arguments for or against a thesis, in offering or refuting a
criticism. In all these cases we do not demonstrate as we do
in mathematics, but we argue. If we conceive of logic as the
study of reasoning in all forms, it is natural that the theory of
demonstration as developed in formal logic should be
accompanied by a theory of argumentation that is similar to
Aristotle's dialectical reasoning. This latter seeks through
argumentation the acceptance or rejection of a debatable
thesis. The object of the new rhetoric, which amplifies as
well as extends Aristotle's work, is thus to study these
arguments and the conditions of their presentation.

Aristotle opposed rhetoric to dialectic when he examined
it in the *Topics,* nevertheless seeing in rhetoric the counter-
part, the *antistrophos,* of dialectic.[11] For him, dialectic is
concerned with arguments used in a controversy or discussion with an individual, while rhetoric concerns the orator's

technique in addressing a crowd gathered in a public square—a group of people who lack both specialized knowledge and the ability to follow a lengthy chain of argument.[12]

In contrast to ancient rhetoric, the new rhetoric is concerned with discourse addressed to *any sort of audience*—a crowd in a public square or a gathering of specialists, a single being or all humanity. It even examines arguments addressed to oneself in private deliberation, or in what is now commonly referred to as "intrapersonal communication." Since it aims to study nondemonstrative discourse, its analysis of reasoning is not limited to formally correct inferences or to more or less mechanical calculations. The theory of argumentation, conceived as a new rhetoric or dialectic, covers the whole range of discourse that aims at persuasion and conviction, whatever the audience addressed and whatever the subject matter. The general study of argumentation can be augmented by specialized methodologies according to the type of audience and the nature of the discipline, should that appear useful. In this manner we can work out a juridical or a philosophical logic that would be the specific application of the new rhetoric to law or philosophy.[13]

In subordinating philosophical logic to the new rhetoric, I am joining in the centuries-old debate which started with Parmenides' great poem and which has set philosophy against rhetoric ever since. The great tradition of Western metaphysics which Parmenides, Plato, Descartes, and Kant represent has always contrasted the search after truth—the announced goal of philosophy—to the techniques of the rhetoricians and Sophists, who have always satisfied themselves with getting people to agree to opinions that are as diverse as they are misleading. Thus Parmenides preferred the road of truth to that of appearance; Descartes based science on unshakable self-evidence, treating what was only probable as all but false; and finally Kant proposed to rid philosophy of opinions altogether by elaborating a metaphysics which is essentially an epistemology, an inventory of all the forms of knowing which, "having an a priori foundation, must be held in advance to be absolutely necessary."

In order to be certain that the propositions articulated by the philosophers did not constitute uncertain and false opinions instead of indisputable truths, it was necessary that these propositions have the benefit of a solid and unquestionable basis—a self-evident intuition that could guarantee the truth of what is perceived as self-evident. The self-evidence so conceived is not a subjective condition, varying from one moment to the next, or from individual to individual; its role is rather to establish a bridge between what is perceived as self-evident by the knowing subject and the truth of the self-evident proposition, which must impose itself in the same way on every rational being.[14]

An argument is never capable of procuring self-evidence, and there is no way or arguing against what is self-evident. Whoever states a self-evident proposition is sure that it will compel everyone with the same "evidence." Argumentation, however, can intervene only where self-evidence is contested. Aristotle had already noticed this; he recognized that it is absolutely necessary to resort to dialectical reasoning when the first principles of a science, which normally are self-evident, are contested.[15] The same thing happens when people dispute a definition.

Although it is normally through intuition that the simple ideas and the first principles of a theoretical science are grasped, Aristotle recognized that recourse to argumentation becomes necessary in practical disciplines such as ethics and politics, where choices and controversies are inevitable, and also in situations where private deliberations or public discussions arise. This is why his *Organon* includes the

Analytics, which is devoted to formal reasoning, along with the *Topics,* which examines the dialectical reasoning which allows for justification of the best opinion, the reasonable opinion, the *eulogos.*

All who believe that they can disengage truth from opinion independently of argumentation have a profound disdain for rhetoric, which relates to opinions; they grant, at best, only a rhetoric which serves to propogate the truths guaranteed to speakers through intuition or self-evidence, but not a rhetoric which seeks to establish these truths. But if we do not concede that philosophical theses can be founded on self-evident intuitions, we must resort to argumentative techniques to make them prevail. The new rhetoric becomes the indispensable instrument for philosophy.[16]

Those who, with Paul Ricoeur, acknowledge the place in philosophy of metaphoric truths which, since they propose a restructuring of reality, cannot prevail through compelling self-evidence, cannot deny the importance of rhetorical techniques in making one metaphor prevail over another.[17] They can disregard such techniques only if they grant the existence of an intuition which would compel a unique vision of reality excluding all others.[18]

The decline of rhetoric since the end of the sixteenth century was due to the rise of European bourgeois thought, which generalized the role of "evidence": the personal "evidence" of Protestantism, the rational "evidence" of Cartesianism, or the sensible "evidence" of empiricism.[19]

The contempt for rhetoric and the eclipse of the theory of argumentation have led to the negation of practical reason, problems of action being sometimes reduced to problems of knowledge, that is, of truth or probability, and sometimes considered as completely irrelevant to reason.

But, if they want to acquire a clear awareness of the intellectual methods that are employed, all who believe in the existence of reasonable choice, preceded by deliberation or discussion where different solutions confront each other, cannot avoid a theory of argumentation such as the new rhetoric presents.

The new rhetoric is not limited to the sphere of practice; it is at the heart of theoretical problems for anyone who is conscious of the roles that are played in our theories by the choice of definitions, models, and analogies—and, in a more general way, by the elaboration of an appropriate language, adapted to the field of our investigations. It is in this sense that the role of argumentation can be conjoined with practical reason; it is a role that is fundamental in all areas in which we perceive the work of practical reason, even when our concern is with the solution of theoretical problems. I want to make this point clear in order to avoid misunderstanding concerning the import of argumentation as I conceive it.[20]

2. Argumentation, Speaker, and Audience

WHAT DISTINGUISHES ARGUMENTATION from formally correct demonstration?

To begin with, a correct demonstration is one that conforms to rules which are made explicit in formalized systems; argumentation, in contrast, flows out of a natural language. Thus, while the signs used in a demonstration are supposed to be completely free from ambiguity, the language upon which argumentation must rely possesses ambiguities that cannot be worked out in advance. This means—and this is the point I wish to stress—that demonstration and argumentation differ over the status of axioms, over the basis from which one starts.

The axioms in a mathematical demonstration are not topics of debate. Mathematicians view them either as true, as self-evident, or as simple hypotheses, and in using them, they generally do not take the trouble to find out whether or not an audience accepts them. Besides, as Aristotle notes in his *Topics,*[1] anyone who needs to justify a choice of axioms should resort to argumentation.

The aim of argumentation is not to deduce consequences from given premises; it is rather to elicit or increase the adherence of the members of an audience to theses that are presented for their consent. Such adherence never comes out of thin air; it presupposes a meeting of minds between speaker and audience. A speech must be heard, as a book must be read, in order to have any effect. Even in private deliberation, where the person who advances reasons and the one who receives them are the same, the meeting of minds is indispensable. Certain maxims flow from this: "Don't listen to the devil in you," or "Laugh at the dark question."

Every society that recognizes the importance of such meetings seeks to organize them and even to make them obligatory. The Sunday mass allows for a weekly meeting between priest and parishoners; compulsory education guarantees teachers the presence of their pupils; the annual convening of parliament specified by the constitution places the government before the elected representatives of the nation; and legal procedures assure the plaintiff the normal course of litigation even if the defendant is recalcitrant.

Ritual, programs of education, parliamentary traditions and rules of procedure fix, with more or less precision, the matters which are the objects of communication. Turning away from them will be considered as illegal or improper, an act of insolence, an object of ridicule or scandal.

I still remember, after thirty years, the painful effect caused by a speaker who, before a crowd, had to deliver some remarks about a deceased friend. He abused the occasion by attacking a member of the crowd. There is similar abuse when a school principal, to whom the education of children conformable to the values of the community has been confided, uses his position to propagate ideas and values which are scandalous.

The establishment or rupture of diplomatic relations constitute preliminaries, signifying that there is a readiness for discussion with the other party or that the other party is not acceptable to us as a spokesman. Before even broaching the question of right in a controversy, it is important to know whether we envisage a settlement of the dispute through negotiation, that is to say, by recourse to argumentation, or by recourse to force.

Argumentation is intended to act upon an audience, to modify an audience's convictions or dispositions through discourse, and it tries to gain a meeting of minds instead of imposing its will through constraint or conditioning. Hence it is not something negligible to be a person to whose opinion we attach some value. Similarly, it is important to be able to speak in certain circumstances, to be the spokesman for a group, institution, or state and to be listened to.

We have seen that every argument presupposes a meeting of minds—a meeting which social and political institutions can facilitate or prevent. It is enough to think of the monopoly of the means of communication that characterizes totalitarian states, and of all the means that are used either to protect or to prevent this meeting of minds. Freedom of speech and the press are important democratic victories, but even in a liberal society not everyone, in whatever circumstances, can speak and make himself heard. Even the most fervent partisan of dialogue is not disposed to engage in a discussion with anyone on any subject whatsoever. Aristotle had already noted this: certain topics, he wrote, not only should not be discussed with just anyone, but should not be debated at all:

> For people who are puzzled to know whether one ought to honor the gods and love one's parents or not need punishment, while those who are puzzled to know whether snow is white or not need perception.[2]

Certain questions do not merit discussion and others cannot be discussed, for even to consider them would be blasphemous or scandalous. Under pain of death, an Athenian decree prohibited discussion of a plan to modify the use of the city's reserve fund.[3] And Pascal, before stating his reasons for belief in the existence of God and the immortality of the soul, spent pages trying to persuade us that the problem is of such importance that it would be insane to neglect it.[4]

We should note in this regard that argumentation does not aim solely at gaining a purely intellectual adherence. Argumentation very often aims at inciting action, or at least at creating a disposition to act. It is essential that the disposition that is created be sufficiently strong to surmount possible obstacles. St. Augustine noted this very aptly in *On Christian Doctrine:*

> When such things are taught that it is sufficient to know or to believe them, they require no more consent than an acknowledgement that they are true. But when that which is taught must be put into practice and is taught for that reason, the truth of what is said is acknowledged in vain and the eloquence of the discourse pleases in vain unless that which is learned is implemented in action. It is necessary therefore for the ecclesiastical orator, when he urges that something be done, not only to teach that he may instruct and to please that he may hold attention, but also to persuade that he may be victorious.[5]

Thus Augustine writes:

> Just as the listener is to be delighted if he is to be retained as a listener, so also is he to be persuaded if he is to be moved to act. And just as he is delighted if you speak sweetly, so is he persuaded if he loves what you promise, fears what you threaten, hates what you condemn, embraces what you commend, sorrows at what you maintain to be sorrowful; rejoices when you announce something delightful, takes pity on those whom you place before him, in speaking, as being pitiful, flees those whom you, moving fear, warn are to be avoided.[6]

Addressing the faithful, urging them to end their internecine wars, Augustine is not satisfied with their praise; he speaks until they begin to shed tears, showing that they are ready to change their attitudes.

These examples prove that when we are dealing with theses presented in an argumentative discourse, these theses aim at times at bringing about a purely intellectul result—a disposition to admit their truth—and at other times at provoking an immediate or eventual action. People who argue do not address what we call "faculties," such as intellect, emotion, or will; they address the whole person, but, depending on the circumstances, their arguments will seek different results and will use methods appropriate to the purpose of the discourse as well as to the audience to be influenced. A lawyer pleading a civil or criminal case will use different styles and kinds of arguments depending on the court he or she has to convince. The only general advice that a theory of argumentation can give is to ask speakers to adapt themselves to their audiences.

What is this audience around which argumentation is centered? Sometimes the answer is obvious. The lawyer who pleads in court must convince the jury or judges who constitute the court. But what about a statesman who addresses Parliament? Is his audience composed of everyone who hears him, even if his address is broadcast? Does the person who is interviewed by a journalist respond to the interviewer, to the readers of the newspaper, or to national or international public opinion? We immediately realize that it is not a question of identifying the speaker's audience with those who are physically capable of listening and, *a fortiori,* with those who would have the chance to read the speaker's words. Besides, we can imagine that the speaker could neglect one part of the audience, e.g. the policeman who attends a hearing, or certain members of the opposition in a political discourse that seeks only to consolidate a parliamentary majority.

The audience is not necessarily made up of those the speaker expressly addresses. In the British Parliament, MPs are supposed to address the Speaker of the House, but in fact they address members of their own party, sometimes seeking thereby to influence national and international opinion. I have seen the following inscription in a village cafe: *"Brave toutou, ne grimpe pas sur la banquette."* ["Nice doggie, don't climb on the bench."] This does not imply that all the dogs let in the cafe can read and comprehend French. If, for the development of a theory of argumentation, we want to define the audience in a useful manner, we must regard it as *the gathering of those whom the speaker wants to influence by his or her arguments.*

What is this gathering? Is is highly changeable. It can be the speaker himself, reflecting privately about how to respond to a delicate situation. Or it may be all of humanity, or at least all those who are competent and reasonable— those whom I would call the "universal audience," which may itself be made up of an infinite variety of particular audiences.

For some people, at once the most individualistic and rationalistic, self-deliberation offers the model of sincere and honest reasoning, where nothing is hidden, no one is deceived, and where one only triumphs over one's own uncertainties. Pascal speaks of "your own assent to yourself, and the unceasing voice of your own reason"[7] as the best criterion of truth. Similarly, Descartes in his preface to the *Meditations* says to the reader: "I shall first present in these Meditations the same thoughts by which I think I have reached a certain and evident knowledge of the truth, in order to see whether I will be able to persuade others by means of the same reasons that have persuaded me."[8]

For certain authors such as Schopenhauer and J.S. Mill, although dialectic is the technique of controversy with another person and rhetoric the technique of public discourse, logic is identified with the rules that are applicable to the conduct of one's own thought.[9] For Chaignet, in his work *La Rhétorique et son histoire,* the distinction between persuasion and conviction consists essentially in that persuasion is a work for others, while one always convinces oneself.[10] But this was before the appearance of psychoanalysis, which may have convinced us that we are capable of deceiving ourselves and that the reasons we give ourselves often amount to nothing more than rationalizations. This idea is found earlier in Schopenhauer, for whom the "intellect" only camouflages the true motives of our behavior, which would be, in themselves, completely irrational.[11]

Since a speaker can use the technique of question and answer to test the idea he forms of another person's convictions and attitudes, the audience made up of a single interlocutor in a dialogue seems to have undeniable advantages over the audience that is made up of a crowd brought together in a public place. Gradually, as the dialogue or controversy develops, the speaker gets to know the interlocutor better and better, for the speaker has the right to assume that the latter is not seeking to lead him astray. The aim of the exchange of ideas is to give the participants a better understanding of each other. The accord that is reached on this occasion guarantees a more closely-woven thread of argument. It is for this reason that Zeno compared dialectic, the technique of dialogue, to a clenched fist, while rhetoric seemed to him similar to an open hand.[12]

The above distinction, which is not without significance, is doubtlessly tied to the better knowledge of the interlocutor in the dialogue, at least with regard to the subject of the debate. It would be pointless for the speaker to develop his argumentation without being concerned with the reactions of his sole interlocutor, who necessarily moves from the role of passive listener to that of active participant.

Someone who prophesies without troubling himself with the reactions of those who hear him is quickly regarded as a fanatic, the prey of interior demons, rather than as a reasonable person seeking to share his convictions. It is therefore not without reason that the Socratic technique of question and answer will appear in this case as suited to argumentation before one person or a small number of people, while long speeches are necessarily given before large audiences. But it is not necessary to transform into a difference of nature a difference of argumentative technique imposed, essentially, by circumstances, and which concerns only the adherence, more or less assured and explicit, to the arguments developed.

Besides, the technique of question and answer is of little value when we are concerned with a presentation on a specialized theme addressed to an audience of experts, in physics, history, or law for example, since each discipline possesses a group of theses and methods which every specialist is supposed to acknowledge and which is rarely called into question. A person cannot arbitrarily contest such theses and methods without betraying his own incompetence, for to do so would be to run counter to the stability of scientific beliefs.[13] The more central such beliefs are to a given discipline, the more serious their abandonment; the more likely it is that their surrender would lead to a scientific revolution, the more recalcitrant those with tenure in the discipline will be in holding them.[14] Sometimes they will yield to the arguments of the revolutionary thinker only after debate has been drawn out over an entire generation.

Thus it is that certain theses and methods are supposed to be recognized by all members of a specialized audience— until a new order is established. It is superfluous to be convinced explicitly of the audience's agreement. It is, on the contrary, in the absence of a body of recognized truths and theses that recourse to a dialectic of question and answer appears to be indispensable.

While the specialist who addresses a learned society and the priest who preaches in his church know the theses upon which they can base their expositions, the philosopher is in an infinitely more difficult situation. In principle, his discourse is addressed to everyone, to a universal audience composed of those who are disposed to hear him and are capable of following his argumentation. Unlike the scholar and the priest, the philosopher does not possess a collection of philosophical theses which are accepted by all the members of his audience. Instead, he searches for facts, truths, and universal values that, even if all the members of the universal audience do not explicitly adhere to them—an impossibility—are nevertheless supposed to compel the assent of every sufficiently enlightened human being. Thus the philosopher appeals to common sense or common opinion, to intuition or to self-evidence, presuming that each member of the universal audience is part of the community to which he alludes, sharing the same intuitions and self-evident truths. Simple denial is not enough to demonstrate a person's disagreement, for if the philosopher's discourse seems generally acceptable and convincing, the recalcitrant would have to prove that he is not mad in opposing common opinions, that there are good reasons to support his opposition or at least his skepticism. Thus, even if a discourse is not addressed to one or a small number of people, but is an appeal to reason—that is, to the universal audience—the necessity for a dialogue that would bear on all controversial points seems unavoidable. This is why dialectic, the technique of controversy, is central to philosophical argumentation as we see it in the Socratic dialogues and in the philosophers inspired by them.

The distinction between discourses which are addressed to a few and those which are valid for everyone allows us better to understand how persuasive discourse differs from discourse that attempts to be convincing. Instead of thinking that persuasion is addressed to the imagination, sentiment, or a person's unthinking reactions, while the convincing discourse appeals to reason;[15] instead of opposing one to the other as subjective to objective,[16] we can characterize them in a more technical and exact way by saying that discourse addressed to a specific audience aims to persuade, while discourse addressed to the universal audience aims to convince.

The distinction thus established does not depend upon the number of persons who hear the speaker, but upon the speaker's intention: does he want the adherence of some or of every reasonable being? It may be that the speaker envisions those to whom he speaks—even in an instance of private deliberation—as the only incarnation of the universal audience.[17] A convincing discourse is one whose premises are universalizable, that is, acceptable in principle to all the members of the universal audience. We immediately realize how in this perspective the originality of philosophy, traditionally associated with notions of truth and reason, will best be understood in its relation to the universal audience and according to the manner in which this audience is understood by the philosopher.

Aristotle centers his *Rhetoric* but not his *Topics* around the idea of the audience. He does this because it is according to the character of the audience that he can examine the passions and emotions which the orator may excite.[18] Thus, inspired by the Athenian practice, he distinguishes three oratorical genres according to the role reserved for the audience:

> Now the hearer must necessarily be either a mere spectator or a judge, and a judge either of things past or of things to come. For instance, a member of the general assembly is a judge of things to come; the dicast, of things past; the mere spectator, of the ability of the speaker.

Therefore there are necessarily three kinds of rhetorical speeches, deliberative, forensic, and epideitic.[19]

In the deliberative genre, the orator advises and dissuades, and he finally recommends what seems the most useful. In the legal or forensic genre, he accuses or defends so as to decide justly upon an issue. In the epideitic genre, he praises or blames, and his speech relates to the worthy and unworthy.[20]

If Aristotle was inspired by political assemblies to describe the deliberative genre, it was the oratorical competitions held during the Olympic Games that inspired the specifics of the epideitic genre. At those games the listeners were the spectators, and if they had some mission to fulfill it was primarily to choose the victor whose speech deserved to carry off the prize:

> The speech was regarded in the same light as a dramatic spectacle or an athletic contest, whose purpose appears to have been to highlight the performers. Because of these special characteristics, the Roman rhetoricians relegated the study of the epideictic to the grammarians, while they trained their pupils in the two kinds of oratory which were deemed relevant to practical eloquence. To the theoreticians, the epideictic speech was a degenerate kind of eloquence, with no other aim than to please, which perforce dealt in embellishments and facts that were certain or at least uncontested. The epideictic genre of oratory thus seemed to them to have more connection with literature than with argumentation.[21]

Yet in my view the epideictic genre is central to discourse because its role is to intensify adherence to values, adherence without which discourses that aim at provoking action cannot find the lever to move or to inspire their listeners. It may even happen that a funeral ceremony, arranged for mourners of a political victim, will degenerate into a riot, requiring that the perpetrators be punished. Analysis of Antony's celebrated discourse in Shakespeare's *Julius Caesar* shows how artificial the distinction of genres really is, because the speaker who seeks to create a unity around certain values in an epideictic discourse—a funeral oration, for example—can take advantage of the created emotion to incite to action, and revolt, those who before the discourse had thought only of gathering around the body of the deceased.

The epideictic discourse normally belongs to the edifying genre because it seeks to create a feeling or disposition to act at the appropriate moment, rather than to act immediately. We would fail to understand the nature or importance of that genre if we were to ascribe to it merely the purpose of gaining glory for the speaker. That can result from the discourse, but we should not confuse the consequence of a discourse with its goal. The goal is always to strengthen a consensus around certain values which one wants to see prevail and which should orient action in the future. It is in this way that all practical philosophy arises from the epideictic genre.

3. The Premises of Argumentation

TO MAKE HIS discourse effective, a speaker must adapt to his audience. What constitutes this adaptation, which is a specific requisite for argumentation? It amounts essentially to this: the speaker can choose as his points of departure only the theses accepted by those he addresses.

In fact, the aim of argumentation is not, like demonstration, to prove the truth of the conclusion from premises, but to transfer to the conclusion the *adherence* accorded to the premises. Lest he fail in his mission, the speaker should depart from his premises only when he knows that they are adequately accepted; if they are not, the speaker's first concern should be to reinforce them with all the means at his disposal. This transfer of adherence is accomplished only through the establishment of a bond between the premises and the theses whose acceptance the speaker wants to achieve. If a conclusion runs totally counter to the convictions an audience holds, the members of the audience will probably prefer to reject one of the premises rather than accept the offending conclusion, and all the speaker's efforts will have been in vain. This result can be compared to the *reductio ad absurdum,* which, ending in a false conclusion, forces us to reject one of the premises as false. In argumentation the problem is equally one of rejection, but one of the premises is rejected not because the conclusion drawn from it is false but because it is unacceptable.

To be unconcerned with the audience's adherence to the

premises of the discourse is to commit the gravest error: *petitio principii* or begging the question. This error, traditionally considered a logical fault, is not a fault of demonstration, because it has nothing to do with the truth or falsity of the propositions that constitute a line of reasoning. The affirmation *if p, then p,* stating that a proposition implies itself, is not only true but is a fundamental logical law: it is the *principle of identity.* But everything changes as soon as we go to the argumentative point of view, because now we are concerned with obtaining, by argumentation, adherence to the thesis *p;* we cannot now initially present it as a thesis already accepted by the audience.

Let me cite an example of *petitio principii,* borrowed from the discourse of Antiphon on the murder of Herodes: "I would like you to know that I am much more deserving of your pity than of punishment. Punishment is indeed the due of the guilty, while pity is the due of those who are the object of an unjust accusation."[1]

The conclusion, given at the start, would follow if the minor premise, "I am innocent," were admitted. In this case the suit would be judged and the accused acquitted. The fact that the case goes on and the judgment is not given immediately proves that we are involved in a *petitio principii.* We can see in this example that it makes sense to distinguish the truth of a thesis from adherence to it. Even if the thesis were true, to suppose it to be accepted while it is yet controversial is to beg the question.

In line with this we should note that Bentham and later Schopenhauer characterized as a *petitio principii* the use, in ostensibly describing something, of terms that either value or devalue it. Bentham called this "begging the question...by the employment of a single appellative."[2] Thus what a neutral observer will think of as a "cultic phenomenon" will be called an "expression of piety" by someone favoring it and an "act of superstition" by someone fighting it.

Bentham's and Schopenahuer's mistake is to see in favorable or unfavorable evaluation a sophism, a *petitio principii,* as if taking a position were, in itself, open to criticism. In fact, one begs the question only to the degree that the position one takes, supposedly shared by the audience, is contested by it. This clarification should help us to see the relativity of begging the question; like all argumentation, it relates to the adherence of the audience. To adapt to an audience is, above all, to choose as premises of argumentation theses the audience already holds.

Among the points of agreement from which the speaker draws the starting point for his discourse, it is important to distinguish those which bear upon *reality* (i.e., facts, truths, and presumptions) from those which bear on the *preferable* (i.e., values, hierarchies, and the *loci* of the preferable).

Although language and common sense designate by the terms "facts" and "truths" objective elements which force themselves upon everyone, an analysis undertaken from an argumentative point of view does not allow us to neglect the attitude of the audience toward these "facts," unless we are prepared to commit a *petitio principii.*

If we accord the status of "fact" or "truth" to an objective element which, according to Poincaré, "is common to many thinking beings, and could be common to all"[3] (i.e., which is supposedly accepted by the universal audience), we could count upon the facts and truths as upon stable data, without concern for reinforcing the audience's adherence to them. "For the individual, adherence to fact will simply be a subjective reaction to something that is binding on everybody."[4]

But as soon as a fact or truth is contested by a member of an audience, the speaker cannot take advantage of it unless he shows that the person who opposes him is mistaken or, at least, shows that there is no reason to take the latter's opinion into account—that is, by disqualifying him, by denying him the status of a competent and reasonable interlocutor.

We see that this status of fact and truth is not guaranteed indefinitely unless we accept the existence of an infallible authority, a deity whose revelations are incontestable and who could guarantee these facts and truths. However, if we lack such an absolute guarantee, such self-evidence, and such necessity as would compel every reasonable being, the facts and truths which are accepted by common opinion or by the opinion of specialists become open to question. However, if there is agreement about their purpose or meaning and the agreement is sufficiently widespread, no one can reject them without appearing foolish, unless he gives adequate reasons to justify his skepticism concerning them. Universalized doubt, such as Descartes extolled, would not serve to disqualify a particular fact because under the circumstances the doubt would not be considered reasonable. Wittgenstein provides pertinent reflection on this subject.[5]

How do we disqualify a fact or a truth? The most effective way is to show its incompatibility with other facts and truths which are more certainly established, preferably with a *bundle* of facts and truths which we are not ready to abandon. At times, this testing can be limited to questioning of the result of an experiment devised with too little care. At other times, however, the testing can lead to an intellectual revolution, scientific, philosophical, or religious in nature. Such confrontation does not necessarily bring forth decisive results. In science, for example, there is a tendency for everyone to adhere to conventional positions, but revolutionary change occurs often under such conditions in philosophical and religious debates.[6]

Along with facts and truths we often depend on presumptions, which, although they are not as certain as our facts and truths, nevertheless furnish a sufficient basis upon which to rest a reasonable conviction. We habitually associate presumptions with what normally happens and with what can be reasonably counted upon.

Although these presumptions, tied to common experience and to common sense, permit one to function reasonably well, they can be contradicted by the facts, because the unexpected can never be excluded.

Let me cite some common presumptions: "the presumption that the quality of an act reveals the quality of the person responsible for it; the presumption of natural trustfulness by which our first reaction is to accept what someone tells us as being true; the presumption of interest leading us to conclude that any statement brought to our knowledge is supposed to be of interest to us; the presumption concerning the sensible character of any human action."[7]

Presumptions are based on the idea that that which happens is normal. But as the idea of normality is susceptible to various interpretations, people get into arguments over whether or not a presumption is applicable to a given set of circumstances, given the facts of the case. Such a dispute would consist in an attempt to overturn a presumption that favored the thesis of one's opponent. This is the most immediate effect of a presumption: it imposes the burden of proof upon the person who wants to oppose its application.

The burden of proof, which is the essential element in legal procedure, refers us to the law, where we can distinguish several kinds of presumptions.

The *presumptions of man* can be both the point of departure and the conclusion of reasoning. On the contrary, *legal presumptions,* established by law or jurisprudence, whether they admit of contrary proof (presumptions *juris tantum*) or are irrefutable (presumptions *juris et de jure*), furnish excellent examples of theses upon which one can base legal reasoning, because in every case they exempt from all proof whose whom they benefit.[8]

We can contrast opinions which are thought to express a known or presumed reality to those which express a preference (values or hierarchies) or which indicate what is preferable (the *loci* of the preferable).

To take Louis Lavelle's definition, we can say that the word "value" applies wherever we deal with "a break with indifference or with the equality of things, wherever one thing must be put before or above another, wherever a thing is judged superior and its merit is to be preferred."[9]

This definition of value is valid, in particular, for hierarchies or where hierarchical elements are expressly indicated. Often, positive or negative values indicate a favorable or unfavorable attitude to what is esteemed or disparaged, without comparison to another object. What is described by the terms "good," "just," "beautiful," "true," or "real" is valued, and what is described as "bad," "unjust," "ugly," "false," or "apparent" is devalued.

Let us take note of the ambiguous expression "reality" or "real." The real, as object of scientific investigation, does not admit of degrees: all realities are on the same level and are compatible with each other. On the contrary, ontology, or the philosophical study of the real, does not hesitate to establish degrees even in the real itself, to structure a hierarchy of aspects, and to mix value judgments with descriptions of the given.

Value judgments, insofar as they are subject to controversy, have been considered by positivist philosophers as completely lacking in objectivity, unlike "reality" judgments about which, thanks to experimentation and verification, universal agreement would be possible. In this view, value judgments serve only as rallying points for special interests. For this reason it would be difficult, without falling into *petitio principii,* to defend the objectivity of values.

Do universal values, such as the true, the good, the

beautiful, and the just, exist? Could we not suggest, without contradiction, that these values are the object of an agreement of the universal audience? These values are the object of a universal agreement as long as they remain undetermined. When one tries to make them precise, applying them to a situation or to a concrete action, disagreements and the opposition of specific groups are not long in coming.

E. Dupréel described universal values as *instruments of persuasion,* "spiritual tools totally separated from the material they mold, prior to the moment of using them, and remaining whole after they are used—ready, as before, to be used again."[10]

Universal values play an important role in argumentation because they allow us to present specific values, those upon which specific groups reach agreement, as more determined aspects of these universal values. This insertion of specific values into a framework which goes beyond them shows that we wish to move beyond specific agreements by recognizing both the importance of the universalization of values and also the importance that we attach to the agreement of the universal audience.

The analysis of the argumentation concerning values must underline the importance of a distinction, which has been too often neglected, between abstract values, such as beauty or justice, and concrete values, such as "La France" or the Church.

Concrete value belongs to a specific being, object, group, or institution, in its uniqueness. To emphasize the uniqueness of a being is to emphasize its value; everything that is interchangeable is devalued. "By revealing to us the unique character of certain beings, groups, or moments in history, the Romantic writers have brought about, even in philosophical thought, a reaction against abstract rationalism, a reaction characterized by the prominent positions assigned to that preeminently concrete value—the human person."[11]

Certain forms of conduct and certain virtues can be defined and comprehended only in relation to concrete values such as fidelity, loyalty, solidarity, and honor. Rationalism and classicism, in contrast, are devoted to abstract virtues, to rules that are valid for everyone and for all occasions, such as justice, truthfulness, love of humanity, the Kantian categorical imperative (where the "moral" is defined as the "universalizable"), and the utilitarian principle of Bentham (which defines the good by what is most useful to the greatest number).

Argumentation cannot do without either abstract or concrete values, but, given the situation, a speaker will subordinate one to the other. Aristotle rated the love of truth, an abstract value, higher than Plato's friendship, a concrete value, while Erasmus saw an unjust peace, a concrete value, to be preferable to justice, an abstract value.

Reasonings about God display this back-and-forth movement of perspectives. Are values valuable because they are derived from God, who is the supreme concrete value, or is God the perfect being because he is the embodiment of the true, the good, and the just? Must we decide, taking God as a model, that a form of conduct is wise and just because it is divine, or that, insofar as it is valued, it must be attributed to God, who cannot commit an evil act? Descartes stated that "to know the nature of God, as far as I was capable of such knowledge, I had only to consider each quality of which I had an idea, and decide whether it was or was not a perfection to possess it. I would then be certain that none of those which had some imperfection was in him, but that all the others were."[12]

Reasoning that is based on concrete values seems characteristic of conservative societies. Abstract values, in contrast, serve more easily as a basis for critiques of society, and can be tied to a justification for change, to a revolutionary spirit.

As well as from values, argumentation also derives support from hierarchies, which can be either concrete or abstract, homogeneous or heterogeneous.

Many arguments begin with the assumption that man is superior to the animals, and gods to men. Max Scheler held that values are hierarchical: values related to men are superior to those that belong to things.[13]

Along with concrete hierarchical values are others that are concerned with abstract values, such as the superiority of the just over the useful. An abstract principle, such as the superiority of cause over effect, can establish a hierarchy among a great number of concrete realities. The superiority of the One over the Many serves as a basis for Plotinus' ontology. While heterogeneous hierarchies relate qualitatively different values (e.g., "the respect for truth is superior to Plato's friendship"), homogeneous hierarchies are based on quantity: preference is given to the greatest quantity of a positive value and, symmetrically, to the smallest quantity of a negative value (e.g., a mild illness is preferable to a severe one).

Although what is opposed to the real and the true can only be appearance, illusion, or error, a conflict of values does not necessarily imply the loss of the sacrificed value. On the contrary, it is because one holds on to what is sacrificed that the sacrifice is painful. A lesser value remains a value nevertheless.

Finally, taking the broadest perspective, we come, in the realm of values, to the *loci* of the preferable, which play a role analogous to presumptions. We can distinguish what the ancients and especially Aristotle called general *loci* and special *loci* ("common topics" and "special topics").[14] But for the purposes of this study, we shall limit ourselves to the *loci* of the preferable that Aristotle examined among the *loci* of accident.[15] In this context, general *loci* are affirmations about what is presumed to be of higher value in any circumstances whatsoever, while special *loci* concern what is preferable in specific situations.

We state the general *loci* of quantity when we assert that what is good for the greatest number is preferable to what profits only a few; that the durable is preferable to the fragile; or that something useful in varied situations is preferable to something that is of use in highly specific ones. If we give as our reason for preferring something that it is unique, rare, irreplaceable, or that it can never happen again *(carpe diem),* we are stating the general *locus* of quality. It is a *locus* that favors the elite over the mass, the exceptional over the normal; that values what is difficult, what must be done at the very moment, what is immediate. The general *locus* quantity characterizes the classical spirit, that of quality the romantic.[16]

Together with the more common general *loci* of quantity and quality we find in our culture recourse to the general *loci* of order, which affirms the superiority of the anterior over the posterior, of cause over consequence; of the existent, which affirms the superiority of what is over what is simply possible; of essence, according superiority to individuals who best represent the essence of the genus; and of the person, implying the superiority of what is tied to the dignity and autonomy of the person.

To illustrate the general *locus* of essence I will cite two examples. Marot speaks to King Francis I:

> King more than Mars by men renowned,
> King the most kingly that was ever crowned...

and Proust uses the same procedure to praise the Duchess of Guermantes:

> ...the Duchess de Guermantes, who, to tell the truth, by dint of being a Guermantes, became to a certain extent something different and more attractive....[17]

It is by virtue of the general *locus* of autonomy that Pascal criticizes diversion: "Is it not to be happy to have a faculty of being amused by diversion? No, for that comes from elsewhere and from without."[18]

In ending this chapter, let us draw attention to the agreements, characteristic of certain arguments, that are due sometimes to the audience one is addressing and sometimes to the unfolding of the discussion itself.

When we address groups which, by their profession or commitment, are supposed to adhere to certain theses, we may assume that as given. The lawyer can assume that the judge is respectful of the country's legislation and of all legal statutes, whatever their origin, as soon as they are recognized in the process of jurisprudence. A scholar who addresses his colleagues can assume that they recognize what constitutes the core of their discipline. The priest in his church can assume that his congregation accepts the authority of the scriptures.

In a dialogue, the proponent of an argument can as he goes along check on the adherence of his interlocutor to the steps of his reasoning. Socrates in his discussion with Callicles says:

> Evidently, then, the case at the moment is this. If at any point in our discussion you agree with me, that matter will have already been adequately tested both by you and by me, and there will no longer be any need to refer to any other touchstone. For you would never have agreed with me through lack of wisdom or excess of modesty, nor again would you agree with me with intent to deceive for you are my friend, as you yourself claim.[19]

Socrates, verifying the explicit agreement of his interlocutor, can move ahead in the dialogue and put his adversary in a bind by leading him into contradiction. This is the distinguishing feature of Socratic irony.

But Socrates does not stop at adherence; he wants more, for he concludes his remarks by saying to Callicles: "In fact, then, any agreement between you and me will have attained the consummation of the truth."[20]

By drawing—a bit hastily—the conclusion that a thesis is true from the fact that they both agree on it, Socrates tries to show that he will not stop at the rhetorician's goal of adherence, but that he wants to reach the philosopher's goal of truth. But this move is possible only at the price of an unwarranted generalization: that their agreement is simply the expression of an objective truth and, as such, of the agreement of the universal audience.

4. Choice, Presence, and Presentation

MODERN CONCEPTIONS OF demonstration, in search of increasing rigor, have come to conceive of proof as relative to a system of which all the elements are explicitly formulated and which, by that very fact, appears isolated from thought in general. It is precisely this attempt at formalization and isolation that makes the system mechanizable and allows a computer to carry out prescribed operations correctly, without the intervention of human thought. Argumentation, however, is part of a process of thought of which the diverse elements are interdependent.

People have tried to systematize and thus give more rigor to branches of nonformal disciplines such as physics or law. These endeavors have been successful, in the process of linking abstract formulas to concrete situations, to the extent that they have not come up against experiments that contradict predictions from the formulas or unforeseen situations that go beyond the preestablished abstract scheme. To adapt the system to experience, to add flexibility to the formulas used, we are obliged to have recourse to argumentation and consequently to reinsert the system within the overall framework of our knowledge and aspirations—to reestablish contact between the field we wanted to isolate and the totality of our convictions and beliefs. This totality, more or less elaborate, more or less fluid, corresponds to a comprehensive vision, whether it be commonsensical or philosophically more sophisticated.

It is from such a totality—from theses accepted by the audience—that the speaker who argues must draw his premises. He will inevitably have to make a choice.

Every argument implies a preliminary selection of facts and values, their specific description in a given language, and an emphasis which varies with the importance given them. Choice of elements, of a mode of description and presentation, judgments of value or importance—all these elements are considered all the more justifiably as exhibiting a partiality when one sees more clearly what other choice, what other presentation, what other value judgment could oppose them. An affirmation and presentation that at first seem objective and impartial appear one sided—deliberately or not—when confronted with evidence from the other side. Pluralism sharpens the critical sense.[1] It is through continual intervention by others that we can best distinguish the subjective from the objective.

This is the test which allows Kant to separate persuasion from conviction, as a belief which has only a subjective foundation from that which is objective. Kant says that

> So long, therefore, as the subject views the judgment merely as an appearance of his mind, persuasion cannot be subjectively distinguished from conviction. The experiment, however, whereby we test upon the understanding of others whether those grounds of the judgment which are valid for us have the same effect on the reason of others as on our own, is a means, although only a subjective means, not indeed of producing conviction, but of detecting any merely private validity in the judgment, that is, anything in it which is mere persuasion.[2]

Kant's reflection recalls Socrates' discourse with Callicles[3] and can be subjected to the same critique: if disagreement with another, equally well-qualified person underscores the subjectivity of our opinion, or at least the fact that it is not accepted by everyone, the agreement of another is not sufficient to guarantee objectivity or even universality, because it may be only an opinion common to a milieu or a given epoch. The test of objectivity and universality must be constantly renewed: the result, however favorable, creates only a presumption of proof, and neither necessity nor obviousness.

Choosing to single out certain things for presentation in a speech draws the attention of the audience to them and thereby gives them a *presence* that prevents them from being neglected. A Chinese tale, told by Mencius, illustrates the effect of presence: "A king sees an ox on its way to sacrifice. He is moved to pity for it and orders that a sheep be used in its place. He confesses he did so because he could see the ox, but not the sheep."[4]

Presence acts directly upon our sensibility. The presentation of an object—Caesar's bloody tunic as brandished by Antony, the children of the victim of the accused—can effectively move the audience or the jury. But effective presence can also lead to problems in that it not only can distract the audience but can also lead them in a direction the speaker did not intend. For this reason the advice of certain teachers of rhetoric, stessing references to physical realities to move an audience, should not always be followed.

But there is more. The techniques of presentation which create presence are essential above all when it is a question of evoking realities that are distant in time and space. This is why it is important not to identify presence as we conceive it, which is presence to consciousness, with effective presence. Recourse to the effects of language and to their capacity to evoke establishes the transition between rhetoric as the art of persuasion and as the technique of literary expression. If rhetoric, according to Bacon, is the art "of applying reason to the imagination for the better moving of the will," it is so, above all, because it combats the domination of our sensibility by our surroundings:

> The affectation beholdeth merely the present: reason
> beholdeth the future and sum of time. And therefore the
> present filling the imagination more, reason is commonly
> vanquished; but after that force of eloquence and persua-
> sion both made things future and remote appear as
> present, then upon the revolt of the imagination reason
> prevaileth.[5]

George Campbell, who was influenced by Hume's asso-
ciationism, gave much space in his *Philosophy of Rhetoric*
(1776) to the conditions of time, place, connection, and
personal interest by which an event affects us and is made
present to our consciousness. The speaker's efforts are to be
praised when he draws attention, through the talent of his
presentation, to events which, without his intervention,
would be neglected but now occupy our attention. What is
present for us is foremost in our minds and important to us.
Curiously, what loses in importance becomes abstract,
almost nonexistent. Certain writers, such as Stephen Spender,
and Arthur Koestler, have observed the way men perceive
reality and how perception is influenced by their sentimental
or political commitments. Spender makes the following
remarks:

> Nearly all human beings have an extremely intermittent
> grasp on reality. Only a few things, which illustrate their
> own interests and ideas, are real to them; other things,
> which are in fact equally real, appear to them as
> abstractions.... Your friends are allies and therefore
> human beings.... Your opponents are just tiresome,
> unreasonable, unnecessary theses, whose lives are so
> many false statements which you would like to strike out
> with a lead bullet.[6]

The tie which is established between the presence to
consciousness of certain elements and the importance we

give them has allowed us to see in rhetoric alone the art of creating this presence, thanks to the techniques of presentation. Richard M. Weaver, in a paper that is considered a classic of American rhetorical theory, said: "But here we must recur to the principle that rhetoric comprehensively considered is an art of emphasis."[7]

The speaker, unlike the logician, ought not enumerate all the links of his reasoning; he can hint at premises which everyone knows, and from this arises the Aristotelian definition of the *enthymeme* as the "rhetorical syllogism."[8] Without doubt, to create presence it is useful to insist at length upon certain elements; in prolonging the attention given them, their presence in the consciousness of the audience is increased.[9] Only by dwelling upon a subject does one create the desired emotions.[10]

Several techniques have been recommended by teachers of rhetoric to achieve this effect: repetition, accumulation of detail, accentuation of particular passages. A subject can at first be treated synthetically, then there can be an enumeration of the parts. Fléchier, in his funeral oration for Henri de La Tour d'Auvergne, Vicomte de Turenne, described the reactions to the Marshal's death:

> What a host of sighs, lamentations, and praises arise from town and countryside! One man, seeing his crops come safe to harvest, blesses his memory.... Another wishes eternal peace to him who ... In one place, one offers a mass for the soul of him who ... In another, a funeral celebration is held for him.... So the whole kingdom weeps for the death of its defender.[11]

This technique for developing a subject has received the name *amplification* in rhetorical theory. We are dealing with a rhetorical figure which utilizes, to create *presence,* the division of the whole into its parts. We will speak of this later as an "argumentative schema."

In another figure, *aggregation,* we begin by enumerating

the parts and end with a synthesis. Vico gives an example: "Your eyes are made for impudence, your face for effrontery, your tongue for false swearing, your hands for plunder, your belly for gluttony...your feet for flight: so you are all malignity."[12]

Similarly, in *synonymy* or *metabole* the same idea is repeated in different words, which seem to correct the thought. In the line from Corneille's *The Cid*, "Go, run, fly and avenge us,"[13] we have an apt illustration.

While the repetition of the same word simply expresses emphasis, *metabole* reinforces this emphasis and accentuates one or another aspect of it. A similar effect can be obtained by *enallage of time,* where, by replacing the future with the present, we realize a marked effect of presence: "If you speak, you *are* dead."

These few examples of rhetorical figures allow us to point out the connection such figures have with the theory of argumentation.

In fact, people commonly use expressions that depart from the ordinary in order to achieve a persuasive effect. Thus it is, according to the *Rhetorica ad Herennium,* that *hypotyposis* [demonstration] is the figure that "sets things out in such a way that the matter seems to unfold, and the thing to happen under our eyes."[14]

For there to be a figure, a person must have before him an expression that is not ordinary and that has a form discernible by a particular structure. In this way repetition constitutes a figure insofar as it is not required by the fact that our interlocutor has not understood us, and interrogation is a figure when it is purely rhetorical, since the speaker already knows the answer to the question. Similarly, *prolepsis* is a useful figure when the speaker presents objections to which he is eager to respond.

A figure is argumentative if its use, leading to a change in perspective, seems normal in relation to the new situation thus suggested. But if the discourse does not gain the audience's adherence, the figure will be perceived as an ornament, a figure of style, ineffective as a means of persuasion. Thus an established metaphor passes unnoticed and even becomes a cliché. Yet a theoretical concept such as Bergson's "duration" is relegated by Sartre to the status of a rhetorical figure, by which he means a simple stylistic ornament, because he rejects it. [15]

What is normal in one context is not in another. Festive clothing is unobtrusive in festive settings. The pseudo-Longinus states:

> No figure is more excellent than the one which is entirely hidden, so that it is no longer recognized as a figure. There is no more wonderful aid and succor in preventing its appearance than sublimity and pathos, for artifice thus enclosed in the midst of something great and dazzling has everything it lacked, and becomes free from any suspicion of deception. [16]

If we think of figures as ornaments added on to the content of discourse, we see only the rhetorical technique of style—flowery, empty, ridiculous ostentation. But since a single and perfectly adequate way to describe reality does not exist, any other way cannot be seen only as a falsification or deformity; the separation between the form and content of discourse cannot be realized in as simple a way as classical thought imagined it. What is the usual and normal manner of expression and what has only literary and ornamental effect cannot be defined once and for all. One may take as normal an expression which passes unnoticed, but this cannot be observed independently of the context, at once linguistic and cultural, of the discourse. Many statements that appear to be simply the expression of the reality one is describing become studied and artificial as soon as they are translated into a foreign language. Equally, a neutral style can be the result of a studied rhetoric. Gide, for example, tried to set forth value judgments that were shocking and out of the ordinary with a flat style that in no way jarred the reader.[17]

We should emphasize that ordinary and common language is a manifestation of the agreement of a community in the same way as are traditional ideas and commonplaces. Agreement on the manner of presenting certain facts—or at least the lack of reserve regarding them—can facilitate the audience's agreement on the substance of a problem. We will see how the simple use of language implies positions which risk being passed over unnoticed if rhetorical analysis is limited to figures alone.

5. Significance and Interpretation of Data

IN A DISCOURSE, all the elements which the speaker conveys can be described only through a language, which must be understood by the audience. Thus the facts called to mind require, beyond their being given, a manner of description and interpretation as well. This does not mean that we adhere to an ontology which neatly separates immediate and irreducible data from theoretically elaborated constructions. Jean Piaget's works on the child's construction of the world clearly show that what to an adult seems given is only the result of a construction made during the early years of life.

The opposition between data and construct is relative from the point of view of argumentation; it enables us to separate the elements which come about through an interpretation from those about which there is an agreement that, until another comes along, is univocal and undisputed. It is appropriate, in this connection, to distinguish 1) the choice between interpretations which, while on a par with each other, are frequently incompatible (as when we ask which train has begun to move—the one we are in or the one next to it); and 2) the choice of a general interpretative scheme by which one proposes to describe reality. The very same action can be described as tightening a bolt; assembling a vehicle; earning a living; assisting the production of a favorable balance of trade.[1] It is possible to describe a phenomenon

isolated from its context. It is also possible to see it as a cause
or an effect, a means or an end, a symbol of a greater whole
or a directive sign. Even when these different interpretations
are not incompatible, acceptance of one casts the others into
the shadows. We are not witnessing a simple objective
expression of reality. We have noted elsewhere that interpretation is not only selection; it can be signification, insertion
into a new context or into an original theory.

As long as the multiplicity of possible interpretations is
not taken into account and the interpretation given has no
rival, there is no inclination to dissociate the data from the
construct. The distinction appears only where a controversy
is raised by a divergence of interpretation.

One meets with the same phenomenon in interpreting a
text. A meaning seems to be given when the text is clear, that
is, when only one reasonable interpretation seems possible.
However, what seems to be a quality of the text may be the
result of ignorance or a lack of imagination. Let us quote
Locke's remark which corroborates this viewpoint:

> Many a man who was pretty well satisfied of the meaning
> of a text of Scripture or clause in the Code, at first
> reading, has by consulting commentators, quite lost the
> sense of it, and, by those elucidations, given rise or
> increase to his doubts and drawn obscurity upon the
> place.[2]

We see precisely how textual clarity is a property that is
relative to the interpreters. It can be ascertained following a
confrontation of points of view, but it cannot be considered
a quality which precedes the confrontation.

The problems of signification and interpretation are
posed in connection with *signs* and *indices*. A sign is a
phenomenon which is capable of evoking what it designates,
to the extent that it is utilized in a communication designated for this evocation. Indices, on the contrary, refer to

things other than themselves, after a fashion that can be called "objective," independently of all [subjective] intention of communication.[3] The markings on trees to guide hikers are signs; traces left by a wild boar in the snow are indices. Linguistic signs are not the only ones we know, but their importance is such that they deserve special study.

A phrase that is spoken so as to communicate a piece of information can betray, through accent, the origin of the person who pronounced it; it is both a sign and an index.

We may wonder whether tracks left on the earth are signs or indices: the soothsayers have seen signs, the expression of the will of the gods, in a congeries of phenomena to which we would not grant the least significance. Although a false interpretation of an index is an error, the erroneous interpretation of a sign can create a misunderstanding, the incomprehension of a message.

For centuries, under the influence of rationalistic thinkers who considered mathematical language the model to be followed by ordinary language, and especially by philosophers, we have lived under the impression that messages, in principle, are clear and that multiple interpretations are the result of their authors' negligence or the interpreter's bad faith. Hence the poor reputation of jurists, especially of attorneys. Contemporary authors such as I.A. Richards have gone to the other extreme. While in the classical tradition we can distinguish the letter from the spirit of the text, the letter itself is seen by Richards as a mirage which dissolves among multiple interpretations. Thus for him as with Jean Paulhan, rhetoric, the technique of expression, is defined as the study of misunderstanding and the ways to remedy it.[4]

Today, it is generally recognized that mathematics and for that matter all formal systems constitute artificial languages that we subject to numerous restrictions in the attempt to eliminate all ambiguity. Such languages represent exceptions to natural languages and hardly are models to be followed in all circumstances. In natural languages, ambiguity—the possibility of multiple interpretations—would be the rule. Specifically, the language of philosophers could only with difficulty do without metaphors which are characterized by their lack of clarity. Nonetheless, it would be extreme to give up the idea that expressions have their proper meanings; such expressions would probably be metaphors that have become common in the language.[5]

Since words alone cannot guarantee infallible comprehension of a message, we must look outside the word: in the phrase, in the verbal or nonverbal context, in what we know of the speaker and his audience. All these factors constitute supplementary information which would permit us to lessen misunderstanding and to comprehend the message according to the intention of the person who gave it. The interpretation, however, must take into account other exigencies, most notably when we are interpreting sacred or legal texts.[6]

Pascal's thought, "when the word of God which is really true, is false literally, it is true spiritually,"[7] adds a further condition to any interpretation of a sacred text: the text must be considered true by the interpreter. To a lesser degree, as soon as an author enjoys a certain standing, people try to interpret his text in such a way that they can consider it true, reasonable, or at least meaningful. But to do this, it will sometimes be necessary to interpret the same sign in two different ways. Heraclitus' celebrated fragment, "we do and do not step twice into the same river," forces us—if we do not want to charge its author with manifest incoherence—to give two different meanings to the expression "the same river," taking this "sameness" to relate in one sense to the banks of the river and in another to the drops of water which make it up.

Similarly, insofar as Article 4 of the Napoleonic Code

requires a judge to give a decision ("the judge who refuses to judge, under the pretext of the silence, the obscurity, or the inadequacy of the law, can be prosecuted as guilty of denying justice"), the judge, *having* to state the law, even in a case not foreseen by the legislator, will have to interpret the texts in such a way that his interpretation will allow him to settle the litigation, even if the customary interpretation offers no solution.

These examples show that if the elimination of all ambiguity is required for the artificial languages logicians and mathematicians use, the use and interpretation of communications in a natural language can be subordinated to other imperatives that make the requirement of univocity only a subordinate condition. Certain ways of using language, such as for poetry, even assume that the speaker must deviate from the usual meaning, since only this deviation from the usual meaning gives the poet's expression the desired affective connotation.[8]

But the normal usage of a language already offers possibilities for multiple options: the interplay of modifying terms, grammatical categories, modalities in the expression of a thought, and relations established between propositions enables us to place the elements of discourse in a hierarchy and to emphasize one or another of their aspects.

A description which seems neutral reveals itself as one-sided when brought up against a different description, the selective character of which is indicated by the use of an *epithet,* of a quality to which one chooses to give prominence. Aristotle has already drawn our attention to this: Orestes is variously described as "the murderer of his mother" and as "the avenger of his father."[9] Each epithet is accurate, but expresses only one aspect of reality.

These modifying terms presuppose previous classifications, for because of these one introduces the described elements into the preconstituted categories. But one can

constitute classes through the conjunctions "and" or "neither."
Associating one element with another brings them together
and tends to place them on an equal footing. This judgment
by association provoked Gide's indignation: "... you should
be as shocked at hearing 'Stirner and Nietzsche' as Nietzsche
himself was at hearing 'Goethe *and* Schiller'."[10]

Gide, however, did not hesitate to use this technique of
association a few pages later:

> One may love the Bible or not understand it, love the
> Thousand and One Nights or not understand it, but, if
> you please, I will divide the whole mass of thinking people
> into two classes, because of two irreconcilable types of
> mentality: those who are moved by these two books, and
> those who are and will remain unaffected by them.[11]

When a reality presents two aspects at the same time, one
can show the preeminence of one of them by qualifying it
with a substantive, the other being mentioned only as an
adjective: there is a world of difference between the description of a person as an "incarnated soul" or as an "animated
body."

The same idea can be formulated affirmatively or negatively;
if negatively, it appears as the refutation of an affirmation
which is made by others but which is consistent enough that
one takes the trouble to refute it. It can, moreover, insinuate,
with outward innocence, that what one denies is not without
reason. Thus Richard Nixon, by repeating again and again
in his campaign for the governorship of California that the
incumbent, Governor Edmund Brown, was not a communist, spread the allegation he claimed to reject.

By subordinating and often even by coordinating propositions, one thereby places them in a hierarchy in the minds of
the listeners. Expressions such as "if not" and "with the
exception of" minimize the very fact they introduce. The
following passage marks the good will of Julian the

Apostate toward the Jews: "They agree with the Gentiles with the exception of their belief in one God. This is special to them and foreign to us. Everything else is common to us both."[12]

What is common is the rule; the exception is of minor importance. In the same way, the grammarian and the stylist draw attention to the importance of the choice of time, modalities of discourse, and the argumentative usage of pronouns, articles, and the demonstrative adjective. In this connection, I refer the reader to *The New Rhetoric,* where all these questions have been examined in greater detail.[13]

6. Techniques of Argumentation

THERE IS A TENDENCY among formalistic logicians to
reduce all deductive reasoning to a demonstration which
would be correct if the operations agreed with a preestablished scheme and incorrect if they did not. Since every
demonstration takes place within a system in which coherence is proven or presupposed and the axioms are
supposed to be true, the truth of the conclusion as demonstrated or its calculable probability is imposed without
discussion. This does not occur when it is a question of
argumentation, as we have shown in the preceding chapters.

Since argumentation concerns theses to which different
audiences adhere with variable intensity, the status of
elements which enter into argumentation cannot be fixed as
it would be in a formal system: this status depends on the
real or presumed adherence of the audience. We have seen
that not only facts and truths can be questioned, but that
even the determination of what the datum is, is contingent
upon the result of a discussion concerning its interpretation,
and, more particularly, concerning the sense and bearing of
the terms used in the description of this datum. Insofar as a
fact can be modified in various ways by inserting it in
categories about which there is no preestablished agreement, a statement concerning it results from a choice which
is always open to discussion.

Contrary to demonstration, which is developed in a well-
defined system, argumentation most often draws upon a

very ill defined *corpus of premises,* and the theses upon which it is based can be partially understood or implicit. While in a demonstration the conclusion can be deduced from premises in a formal manner, arguments which are given in support of a thesis do not necessarily entail it. They are more or less strong, as are the arguments that are presented for the opposing thesis. People will subscribe to one or the other competing theses, depending upon their appraisal of the arguments which are given *pro* and *contra* and the value of the solution they offer to the problems under discussion.

Argumentation, in its most complete elaboration, forms a discourse wherein the points of agreement upon which it is founded, as well as the arguments advanced, can be addressed, simultaneously or successively, to different audiences. Not only do these arguments interact upon each other; the audiences can, in addition, take these arguments and their relation to the speaker as the object of a new argumentation. It will be necessary to analyze the discourse in its totality when we deal with the fullness of argumentation and the order of arguments in the discourse. Before we go to the synthetic study, let us analyze the different types of arguments and their specific qualities.

Arguments are sometimes given in the form of a *liaison,* which allows for the transference to the conclusion of the adherence accorded the premises, and at other times in the form of a *dissociation,* which aims at separating elements which language or a recognized tradition have previously tied together.

The question as to whether we have a liaison between separate elements or an already preexistent unity will be determined by the speaker's expressions. This does not mean that the speaker may not hesitate in organizing these elements. Bossuet, for example, thought of how to describe the sorrowful death of a sinner as a consequence of his bad life; then, upon reflection, he conceived of life and death as constituting an undeniable unity: "Death has no distinct being which separates it from life; it is nothing but a life coming to an end."[1]

We will examine three types of liaisons in the following chapters: quasi-logical arguments, arguments which are based on the structure of reality, and arguments which establish this structure.[2]

Quasi-logical arguments are those which can be understood by way of comparison to logical, mathematical, formal thinking. However, a quasi-logical argument differs from formal deduction in that it always presupposes adherence to nonformal theses which alone allow the application of the argument.

Let us take the *argument by division,* wherein we draw a conclusion about the whole after we have reasoned about each of the parts. A lawyer, for example, tries to show that the accused, having acted out of neither jealousy, hate, nor cupidity, had no motive for murder. This line of reasoning recalls the division of a surface into parts: what cannot be found in any of the parts cannot be found in the subdivided space. To ensure the validity of the argument, the enumeration of the parts must be exhaustive. Quintilian remarked: "If we omit a single hypothesis in our enumeration, the whole edifice falls to the ground and we invite ridicule."[3]

This argument necessitates a "spatialized" structure of reality, as it were, from which are excluded overlappings, interactions, and fluidity, which characterize concrete situations. To use this type of argument, one must necessarily reduce reality to a logical or mathematical schema on which to reason while nonetheless transposing the conclusion to concrete reality.

Arguments that are based on the structure of reality depend on liaisons which exist among the elements of reality. Belief in the existence of such objective structures can be conveyed to varied realities: relations of causality, or essences of which certain phenomena are only the manifestation. What is important is the existence of agreements which are not questioned and which the speaker uses to develop his argumentation.

Here is how Bossuet uses a structure of reality which is consistent with Christian tradition, to which he draws the attention of the faithful in order to increase their respect for the words of preachers:

> The temple of God, Christians, has two august and venerable places, I mean the altar and the pulpit.... There is a very close alliance between these two holy places, and the things that are transacted in them have a wonderful relationship.... It is because of this wonderful relationship between altar and pulpit that some ancient divines did not hesitate to preach to the faithful that they ought to approach both of them with equal veneration.... That man is no less blameworthy who listens carelessly to the holy word than he who by his own fault lets fall the very body of the Son of God.[4]

Because of the bond between altar and pulpit, Bossuet could ask the faithful to show the same respect for the pulpit that they show for the altar. The bond that exists between them favors this transfer of attitude.

Arguments which establish the structure of reality are those which, starting from a known specific case, allow the establishment of a precedent, model, or general rule, such as enable reasoning by model or example. It is in this same category that we will examine the different types of arguments by analogy which serve sometimes to structure an unknown reality, and sometimes to take a position in regard to it. The use of metaphor will be examined, not from a poetic but from a rhetorical perspective, showing to what degree metaphorical expression orients thought.

The argumentative technique which has recourse to *disso-ciation* hardly attracted the attention of the theoreticians of ancient rhetoric. However, it is fundamental for every reflection which, seeking to resolve a difficulty raised by common thought, is required to dissociate the elements of reality from each other and bring about a new organization of data. By dissociating, among elements described in the same way, the real from the apparent, we move in the direction of elaborating a philosophical reality which is opposed to the reality of common sense. [5]

Because dissociations are central in all original philo-sophical thought, pairs created by this technique will be called "philosophical pairs," as opposed to "antithetical pairs," such as good and evil, and to "classificatory pairs," such as animal/vegetable or north/south.

We will end our analysis with a study of discourse in its totality and with an examination of the problems which are raised by the fullness of discourse, and by the strength and order of arguments.

7. Quasi-Logical Arguments

WE WILL CLASSIFY quasi-logical arguments by comparing them to formal reasoning, with which they have something in common; then we will have to draw attention to the things that distinguish them from formal reasoning, that is, to the things which give rise to controversy and thereby make them nonrigorous. In order to transform an argument into a rigorous demonstration, a person would have to define all the terms used, eliminate all ambiguity, and remove from the argument the possibility of multiple interpretations. Thus, although every nonspecialist will be struck by the logical appearance of quasi-logical arguments, the specialist in formal logic will immediately spot everything that differentiates such arguments from rigorous deduction.

The quasi-logical argument's lack of rigor and preciseness may seem to be a logical flaw, but to charge a person with using a logically flawed argument would make sense only if that person claimed to advance a logical demonstration. The reasons a speaker develops in favor of a thesis are of another sort; they are not instances of correct or incorrect demonstrations, but of stronger or weaker arguments that the speaker can reinforce if necessary with arguments of other kinds.

Let us note in passing that in antiquity, when the mathematical version of scientific thinking was less developed, recourse to quasi-logical arguments was more frequent. Today our first reaction is to emphasize the weakness of such arguments by comparing them with formal structures.

1. Contradiction and Incompatibility

The assertion, within a formal system, of a proposition and of its negation—that is, of a contradiction—makes the system incoherent and hence unusable. In this case the system must be modified so as to eliminate the possibility of simultaneously affirming that a statement is both true and false. It is necessary to choose one or the other affirmation.

However, this solution is not imposed upon us when we are faced with a contradiction that is stated in ordinary language. We have seen from the well-known fragment of Heraclitus ("We step and do not step twice into the same river") that we react to many seeming contradictions by observing that they are only *apparent*. In this case we get rid of the contradiction by interpreting "the same river" in two different ways, so that the affirmation can be true on the first interpretation and the negation true on the second.

When the signs used are univocal, there is no escape through a *distinguo,* and the contradiction leads to absurdity. But this does not happen with expressions in a natural language. At best, natural expressions can only be presumed to be univocal, but this presumption disappears before another, namely, the presumption that the person who speaks to us does not utter patent absurdities.

Thus, in argumentation we find ourselves faced not with contradictions but with incompatibilities in those instances in which the affirmation of a rule, assertion of a thesis, or adoption of an attitude involves us, even against our will, in a conflict with either a previously affirmed thesis or rule, or with a generally accepted thesis to which we as members of a group are expected to adhere.

One example of incompatibility is that of the teacher who teaches children that they must obey their parents and that they must not lie. What happens when the father orders the child to lie or when the father and mother give irreconcilable orders? Another example is the person who assumes it is wrong to kill a living being, yet is shown that by curing a purulent abscess he will kill a multitude of microbes. We can see that incompatibility forces a person to choose, to indicate, in a conflict, which rule will be followed and which relinquished or at least restricted in its scope.

A person becomes laughable when forced into an incompatibility without being aware of it. Laughter penalizes his blindness.[1] Ridicule is a powerful instrument in controversy, and Socrates did not hesitate to use it in his dialectic. "He would be equally ridiculous who, forced to admit an incompatibility, seems, by his behavior, to avoid a choice or an arrangement by compromises."[2]

The fear of ridicule and of the disrepute it involves is an effective means of argumentation—and of education. To preserve the esteem of others, a person will try to avoid ridicule at all costs. A wise person will not lightly advance an erroneous proposition because he would risk ridicule. Even a person who alters his opinion would be ridiculous if he were unable to justify his change of attitude.

Let us note, however, that a person can brave ridicule by making a show of his authority. The outcome of this conflict is, of course, uncertain. For Isocrates, a leader's prestige is measured by his ability to impose seemingly ridiculous rules and nonetheless obtain the submission of his subordinates.[3] If one dares to resist facts and reason, it is best to do so with the backing of divine prestige: by the *credo quia absurdum* Tertullian expressed the supernatural character of his faith.

Normally, although incompatibilities are presented in order to be solved, the solution is not given in advance. International private law has developed exclusively to resolve conflicts of law occassioned by the interference in a system of law of laws which are foreign to that system, but whose application the system imposes.

Paragraph 3 of Article 3 of the Napoleonic Code says: "Laws concerning the state and capacity of persons govern the *French,* even those residing abroad." Jurisprudence deduces from this by symmetry that the state and capacity of foreigners in France are governed by their national laws. But what is to be done in the case of a divorce between two married people of different nationalities, when the national law of one spouse authorizes divorce while that of the other forbids it? The incompatibility results from the simultaneous application, prescribed by the law, of two systems which, when existing in separate jurisdictions, offer no particular difficulty.

Conflict can result from a human decision. The head of a government who asks for a vote of confidence asserts that there is an incompatibility between the rejection of his proposition and his remaining in power. The conflict, though it results from a human decision, must be treated as if it were a law of nature, once it seems unavoidable.

What La Bruyère says about two women who detest each other can also be applied to states at war:

> Neutrality between women toward whom one is equally friendly, although they have broken with each other for reasons that have nothing to do with us, is a difficult matter: often we must choose between them, or lose them both.[4]

Two groups, such as the Catholic Church and the Communist Party, can decide either that membership in one is incompatible with membership in the other or that both are compatible. It can even be that leaders of these groups have opposing attitudes on this subject.

The way that rules are presented and situations described

determines whether they appear compatible or incompatible. If one of two rules which are mutually exclusive is always applicable, conflict is inevitable; but they again become compatible if there is a division in time, in space, or in respect to the object, which allows avoidance of conflict. "Two assertions by the same person at different times in his life can be presented as incompatible if all the statements of that person are regarded as forming a single system; if the different periods of his life are regarded as not being intimately connected with one another, the incompatibility disappears."[5] It would be the same with statements made by different members of a group, depending on whether or not they are considered representatives of the group.

Among the innumerable cases of incompatibility are those which result not from two different rules that oppose each other, but from the assertion that a rule is incompatible with the conditions or the consequences of its assertion or application. Such incompatibilities are called *autophagia*. *Retort* is the argument which attacks a rule by making *autophagia* evident.[6]

A comic example of retort allows us to understand the mechanism of this form of reasoning. In a provincial theater, when the public began to sing the *Marseillaise,* a policeman climbed on the stage to announce that it was forbidden to do anything which was not on the playbill. "How about you," asked one of the spectators, "are you on the playbill?"[7] This example shows an application of *autophagia* and how to avoid retort: it would suffice to exempt public officials from the regulation. The structure of *autophagia,* clearly revealed in this episode, occurs whenever there is recourse to retort.[8]

Aristotle showed that whoever objects to the principle of noncontradiction can be refuted by retort: a person who rejects noncontradiction must nonetheless rely upon it if he wishes to claim that someone defending the principle is wrong. His action in objecting to the principle implies what his words deny. The argument is not purely formal, because to show the incompatibility it is necessary to formulate what rejection of the principle of noncontradiction presupposes; but this formulation could become an object of controversy.

Another situation leading to *autophagia* occurs when an attempt to apply a rule to itself is unsuccessful. For example, when neo-positivists assert that every meaningful proposition is either analytical or empirical, one can ask if this proposition is meaningful, and, if so, whether it is analytical or based on experience.

An additional form of *autophagia* opposes an assertion to the conditions and consequences of its application. Here is a message left by a lawyer for his domestic: "I went to the restaurant *A l'elephant,* where you can find me. If you can't read, take this note to the librarian, who will read it for you."[9] To Epicurus, who advised a sage not to have children and not to recognize them if he did, Epictetus ironically replies, "Why, I think that if your father and mother had foreseen that you were going to talk thus, even then they would not have cast you away from them."[10] The aim of Epictetus' remark is to ridicule Epicurus, for if his parents had followed his advice, they would not have given him birth or else would have abandoned him, had they been Epicurean sages. We can clearly see from these examples that *autophagia* does not lead to the absurd but to the ridiculous.

Since incompatibility, as opposed to formal contradiction, is not universal but comes about only in specific situations, escape consists in examining in advance all situations which can bring it about. This is the *logical* attitude of the jurist or Talmudist who imagines the most varied situations which could raise difficulties and seeks to resolve them in advance.

A discussion among Talmudists concerned the rule according to which a pigeon, found less than a certain distance from the coop, is supposed to belong to the owner, and beyond this distance to whomever finds it. An impertinent rabbi stood up and asked, "What happens when one foot is found at a lesser distance and one at a farther distance?" The Talmud records that there was no response, but that the rabbi was chased from the Academy (*Baba Batra,* 230).

The Academy's attitude suggests that there are cases which we refuse to consider so as not to have to settle beforehand marginal cases whose solution ought to depend upon the context. This is the *practical* attitude of the person who refuses to attempt to solve in advance all problems which can arise. Prudent judges, when they must decide delicate cases, are forced to limit the scope of the ruling which made their disposition possible, so as not to create a precedent that would bind future judges, who will probably have to examine somewhat different cases.

Whoever does not what to sacrifice a rule or even dispose of an incompatibility which has arisen at an inopportune moment will arrange it so that the delicate situation does not show itself and the incompatibility does not have to be raised. This is the *diplomatic* attitude.

Proust, citing Saint-Simon, described at length the subterfuges to which the nobility resorted so as not to have to settle the delicate problems of precedence.

> In certain cases, in view of the impossibility of arriving at a decision, a compromise is arranged by which the son of Louis XIV, Monseigneur, shall entertain certain foreign sovereigns only out of doors, in the open air, so that it may not be said that in entering the house one has preceded the other.[11]

One sees to it that the problematic situation does not arise or, if it does, pretends not to see it by falling back on silence, make-believe, or even lying.

It is a custom in Japan to receive visitors only in proper dress. If a visitor surprises his host while he is at work, he pretends not to see him and greets him only after his host has changed his clothes. "Diplomatic sickness" is one of the techniques that allows for delay in making a disagreeable choice or a painful sacrifice, but at the cost of a lie. In this respect we cite Jankelevitch's comparison of almsgiving and lying: "Almsgiving, like telling a lie, pushes the problem away without solving it, makes the difficulty greater by postponing it."[12]

This is why if we want to resolve an incompatibility and not just put it off, we must sacrifice one of the two conflicting rules, or at least "recast" the incompatibility by a dissociation of ideas. Later, we will go into detail about this technique of reasoning, which is essential to argumentation.

2. Identity, Definition, Analycity, and Tautology

A purely formal identity is self-evident or is posited by convention, but in any case it escapes controversy and hence argumentation. Yet this is never the case with identifications which we come across in ordinary discourse. These aim sometimes for a complete identity and at other times for a partial identity of the elements involved.

The identification of two expressions can result from definition or from analysis.

In the process of defining a term, the claim to identify the defining expression (the *definiens*) with the term to be defined (the *definiendum*) constitutes an argumentative, quasi-logical usage of identity. Indeed, unless a person particularly emphasizes the fact that the defining expression gives only an approximation, the definition will tend to view as interchangeable the defined term and the expression which defines it.

Let us distinguish four kinds of definitions in ordinary language: (1) normative definition, which prescribes the usage of a term; (2) descriptive definition, which indicates normal usage; (3) condensed definition, which shows the essential elements of the descriptive definition; and (4) complex definition, which combines, in various ways, elements of the preceding definitions.[13]

Logicians tend to consider definitions as arbitrary; but this is true only in a formal system where signs are supposed to have only the meaning which is attributed to them by convention. It is never true in ordinary language, except in the case of scholarly or scientific words (i.e. neologisms) which are introduced into the language with a given meaning. If a word already exists, its definition can never be considered arbitrary, for the word is bound up in the language with previous classifications, with value judgments which give it, in advance, an affective, positive or negative coloration. Indeed, if it were otherwise, we could not understand the constant discussion about the meanings of words we find in the Platonic dialogues. If we attempt to give a descriptive definition, it can be put to the test of experience, as can any usage. If, on the other hand, it is a question of a normative definition of a word such as "justice" or "democracy," which designates an idea to which value is attached, one does, through definition, transfer to the *definiens* the value attributed to the *definiendum*. It is understandable that such a transfer, specifying to what the value must be attributed, cannot be the object of an arbitrary decision, for such an arbitrary transfer would use an appeal to authority to cut short a dispute over values.[14]

It is for this reason that in philosophy the definition of a disputed value must be justified by argumentation, because to admit the definition of such a value is to acknowledge the quasi-logical argument by which the *definiendum* and the *definiens* are considered interchangeable. In defining an idea that has a habitual usage in a language, we identify, by means of a definition, the proposed definition with the habitual meaning of the idea; this cannot be the object of an arbitrary decision.

Every time an idea can be defined in more than one way, "to define" comes to mean to make a choice, which could be admissible without discussion only if its consequences were negligible for the processes of reasoning. If, on the contrary, a definition orients reasoning, it must be justified. A legal definition can be imposed only if one has the authority of the legislator at his disposal.

Insofar as an analytic judgment is one which results from linguistic conventions, one can immediately see that one can assimilate to it every equivalence that is based on a definition. The assertion, central to modern neo-positivism, that every logical law is analytical results from the identification of logic with a language established by convention, such as the language has been determined by the axioms of the system and the allowed rules of deduction. A reflection on the status of logic will examine the validity of the identification of logic with a language and the philosophical presuppositions of such an identification. Does this identification result from an arbitrary definition? If not, we can take up, regarding the idea of analycity, the preceding remarks on definition.

The name "analytical philosophy" has been given to the philosophical movement that has come from the Oxford school. In its view, the task of philosophy consists in linguistic analysis. Professor John Wisdom distinguishes three types of analyses: *material, formal,* and *philosophical.*[15] Material analysis is limited to explaining one or the other of the employed terms: "A is the child of B" means that "A is the son or daughter of B." Formal analysis clarifies the logical structure of the proposition, as in Bertrand Russell's well-known analysis which points out that the phrase "The king of France is bald" is equivalent to saying "There is one and only one being who is king of France and who is bald." While these two analytical forms are of a linguistic or logical nature, philosophical analysis goes from the complex to the simple, to the final elements, be they fundamental facts or sense data.

L.S. Stebbing called the analytical method "directional."[16] But looked at from the viewpoint of argumentation and not from that of ontology, all analysis is directional, for it aims to make certain expressions interchangeable by leading the audience toward conceptions that conform to what the speaker has in mind and by setting aside different interpretations another person might want to give to the statements being analyzed. For example, Russell's analysis has been disputed by Strawson, who has emphasized the obvious presuppositions in the use of ordinary language which Russell's analysis tries to conjure away: according to Russell, the proposition "the king of France is bald" is false if there is no king of France when one utters the phrase, while for Strawson, the proposition in these conditions is not false but lacks application: "The question does not arise."[17] In the same way directional analysis makes use of a quasi-logical argument to reduce a complex expression to only those ontological elements of which the speaker feels certain, by considering as negligible all the aspects by which the statement could differ from the elements into which the analysis reduces them. By means of different philosophical techniques, analysis leads to the same argumentative consequences as definition.

Analysis, like definition, could claim a status different from that of quasi-logical argumentation. While definition, to be free from controversy, is posited as arbitrary, analysis will be presented as self-evident and necessary. But in this case couldn't we make the contrary reproach—knowing we are learning nothing new, analysis completely fails to interest us, because it is *tautological?* It only recaptures the contents of the analyzed proposition in other terms, that is, by recourse to a definition. The tautological character of analysis is thus at one with the noncontroversial status of the definition.

Certain expressions, such as "Business is business" or "A penny saved is a penny earned" seem indisputable tautologies. In reality, however, they are only *apparent* tautologies: although they are presented as statements of identity, those who interpret them try to make the statements mean something worth saying by differentiating the terms which are said to be identical.

As with the contradiction that is transformed by interpretation into an apparent contradiction, tautology is transformed into apparent tautology by giving the two terms different meanings.

> But it would be incorrect to think that the exact meaning of the terms is fixed in advance or that the relation between the terms is always the same. The formulation of an identity puts us on the track of a difference, but does not specify to what we should set our attention.[18]

It is the responsibility of the one who reads or hears an apparent tautology to interpret it in the most appropriate way. Marcel Jouhandeau related this charming example: "When I see everything I see, I think what I think."[19]

Several rhetorical figures use tautologies and apparent contradictions to cause several meanings to adhere to the same word.[20]

3. Reciprocity and the Rule of Justice

Leibniz defines two beings as identical if every statement concerning one is equivalent to a statement concerning the other. It would therefore be rational to treat identical beings in the same way because there would be no reason to treat them differently.

The principle which considers two identical beings as interchangeable can be easily accepted because there is little chance that it could ever be applied. Are there identical beings? The German logician Gottlob Frege was able to show that we never identify as identical two different beings but only two different ways of designating the same being. For example, we show that the morning star is identical to the evening star, thus proving that these different expressions point to the same celestial body.[21] In practice, the problem is to know in what case it is rational or just to treat in the same way two beings or situations which differ but which can be likened to each other. It is thus a question of partial, not complete identification, which is justified by the fact that the differences are considered negligible but the likenesses essential.

What is or is not negligible depends upon the desired end. In fact, when we have to establish correlations between phenomena so as to be able to foresee, with an adequate degree of probability, that a phenomenon of type A will be accompanied or followed by a phenomenon of type B, it is experimentation (eventually explained theoretically) which allows us to determine which aspects of the phenomenon can be neglected in elaborating classifications and in searching for regularities or natural laws.

On the contrary, when it is a question of elaborating rules of conduct determining which obligations ought to be imposed on all individuals who find themselves in a given situation, and what obligations we have to such rules—in other words, when it is a question of normative and not simply of descriptive laws—the essential or negligible character of some characteristic or other depends upon the ends the rule intends to pursue. The generally accepted principle of equality before the law means that *everyone* who possesses characteristics that are stipulated by the law will be treated in the same way, that is, in the manner determined by the law.

This principle is a purely formal rule of justice according to which "beings in the same essential category should be treated in the same way."[22] To follow precedent, in the absence of important reasons for putting it aside, is only an application of this rule of justice. The latter is only the expression of a principle of inertia, which shows that in an analogous situation it is reasonable to react in the same way as we did previously, if we had no reason for regrets. Customs are born in this way and give a normative value to a habitual course of action.

We normally find it unjust, because characterized by partiality, to behave differently in two comparable situations. Demosthenes offers an example of the use of justice in argumentation: "Would they claim, perhaps, that a treaty which is unfavorable to our city is binding, and yet refuse to recognize it if it gives us any guarantees? Do you find this just?"[23]

The rule of justice and the recourse to precedent which results from it can be subject to two criticisms. The first deals with the problem of the assimilation of two essentially different situations. Here is a passage from a novel by the Romanian author C. Virgil Gheorghiu, in which one of the characters seems to protest the equal treatment of prisoners:

> Of the fifteen thousand prisoners shut up with me, three thousand no longer have whole bodies. About two hundred have no legs at all. They drag about camp like reptiles. Twelve hundred prisoners have only one leg, others are one-armed. A few have both arms missing. So much for the external parts of the body....
>
> These fractions of men who retain only a given proportion of their bodies receive the same quantity of food as prisoners in possession of their full quota of limbs. This is

a great injustice.

I propose that these prisoners should receive rations in proportion to the amount of body still in their possession.[24]

Gheorghiu's macabre humor stands in revolt against the loss of individuality caused by the insertion of men into the most varied types of bureaucratic categories. His irony suggests new categories and seeks to evoke a revulsion toward this extreme contempt for the human being. But a person would not reason differently if he seriously tried to replace one essential category with another, suggesting, for example, that men be treated according to their needs and not according to their works.

The second criticism concerns the treatment accorded two situations that are equated with each other. Locke is surprised that we do not leave it to each man to seek, in his own way, the salvation of his soul, since we allow him to manage his own patrimony as he pleases.[25] Locke wants the same liberalism applied to religious matters as is applied to civil matters. But today, when there is greater and greater regulation of the economy, equation of the two situations could produce the opposite effect, leading, in the realm of conscience, to a growing intervention by public powers similar to that which takes place in the economy.

The argument of reciprocity equates two beings or situations, by showing that correlative expressions in a relation ought to be treated in the same fashion. In formal logic, the terms A and B, antecedent and consequent of a relationship, R, can be inverted without difficulty if the relationship is symmetrical. In showing this symmetry to be essential, we can claim that it is necessary to equate the terms and that there is reason to apply to them the rule of justice which demands equal treatment.

Here are several examples drawn from ancient and modern sources: "What is honorable to learn is also honorable to teach"[26]; "If it is no disgrace for you to sell them, it is no disgrace for us to buy them."[27] La Bruyère is surprised to see "a crowd of Christians of both sexes who gather on certain days in a hall to applaud a troupe of excommunicants who exist as such only by virtue of the pleasure which they give."[28] Similarly, an indignant beggar is reported to have said: "I don't understand how begging can be a crime in a society where charity is a virtue."[29]

The Golden Rule, in many forms, results from the application of the rule of justice to situations which are claimed to be symmetrical. "Do not do to another what you would not have done to you." Isocrates praises the Athenians by saying: "They require of themselves toward their inferiors the same feelings they ask of their superiors."[30]

The application of the argument of reciprocity, through the reversal of situations which it brings about, causes us to reflect on the strangeness of our own mores, although we consider them normal because we are accustomed to them. To this we owe the educational effect of tales such as Montesquieu's *Persian Letters* which invite us to view our own customs and institutions with the eyes of strangers. I also remember a humorous sketch in which the owner of two cats was taking his bath in his tub when one cat said to another: "Why doesn't he lick himself like everyone else does?"

Recourse to the argument of reciprocity becomes truly comical, and even scandalous, when the equation of situations neglects their essential differences:

At Surat an Englishman is pouring out a bottle of ale which is foaming freely. He asks an Indian, who is amazed at the sight, what he finds so strange. "What bothers me," replies the native, "isn't what is coming out of the bottle, but how you got it in there in the first place."[31]

Lawrence Sterne, who creates numerous comic effects

from the parody of argumentation, relates the following dialogue:

> But whoever thought, cried *Kysarcius,* of laying with his grandmother?——The young gentleman, replied *Yorick,* whom *Selden* speaks of——who not only thought of it, but justified his intention to his father by the argument drawn from the law of retaliation——"You lay'd, Sir, with my mother, said the lad——Why may I not lie with yours?"[32]

The law of retaliation, which applies to punishment the same rule of justice which the Golden Rule applies to moral conduct, is inapplicable when the symmetry is only apparent, whether the reason is the intervention of a natural phenomenon, a familial relationship, or a personal attitude which prevents the equation of situations, as in this account by Jouhandeau:

> "Levy, if I had known you were so rich, I would not have loved you. But you, rather than Raymond, would have married me; and I would have betrayed you with him until, by dint of stealing from you, when we would have been able to be happy together without you, I would have left you. But everything happened otherwise. I am his wife, and even if you were richer than you are, neither for gold nor for silver would I betray Raymond with you."[33]

In certain cases the validity of the equation can be questioned. What is the persuasive force of this thought of Montaigne: "It is as foolish to lament that we shall not be alive a hundred years from now as it is to lament that we were not alive a hundred years ago"?[34] Should we compare the time when we shall be dead to the time when we were not yet born? Should we likewise consider that beings who were born must necessarily die, and draw from this the conclusion that the immortality of the gods is incompatible with the fact that they were born into the world? These and other examples where arguments of reciprocity are applied to reality show the quasi-logical aspect of reasoning which constitutes the rule of justice in situations considered to be symmetrical.

4. Arguments of Transitivity, Inclusion, and Division

Transitivity is the formal property of a relationship which allows the affirmation that if a certain relation exists between the first term and a second, between the second and a third, then the same relation exists between the first and the third. This property characterizes relations such as "equal to," "included in," and "greater than." The relationship $a Rc$ is always true if the premises $a Rb$ and $b Rc$ are true. But there are cases when transitivity is claimed without always being valid. "The friends of my friends are my friends" asserts an argumentative transitivity which can be contradicted by experience. A person proclaiming this adage could defend it, in spite of invalidating cases, by declaring that it is true for *genuine* friends. Thus, defining "genuine friendship" as transitive, the adage is transformed into an analytical proposition which no experience can refute.

The syllogism affirms the transitivity of the relation of inclusion or implication. When these relations are defined in a formal system, the transitivity is not open to doubt. But is it the same in the Chinese *sorites,* where the phrase that constitutes the second part of a proposition is taken up again at the beginning of the following proposition, each time linking the desired end to the means of achieving it? Here is an example from the *Ta Hio:*

The Ancients, who desired intelligence to play its educative role through the whole country, first established order in their own principality; desiring to establish order in their own principality, they first regulated their family life; desiring to regulate their family life, they first improved their own characters; desiring to improve their own characters, they first purified their hearts; desiring to purify their hearts, they sought for sincerity in their thoughts; seeking for sincerity in their thoughts, they applied themselves first to perfect knowledge; this perfect knowledge consists in acquiring a sense of reality.[35]

Does this movement from consequence to condition, which, if inverted, would give a symmetrical movement from conditions to consequences, present as an enthymeme a compelling transitivity or rather an argumentation which owes its appeal to the single form it adopts? In any case, we are far from the formal transitivity from which follows the existence of a property common to all the elements connected by it.

The inclusion of the part in the whole allows us to say that the whole is greater than any of its parts. What is a demonstrated truth in arithmetic or geometry becomes a quasi-logical argument if we draw from it such typical consequences as "the whole is worth more than a part," or "what is not permitted to the whole is not permitted to the part"; or again, "who can do the most can do the least," where "the least" is considered a part of the whole, which is "the most." Locke implicitly used this type of argument in the following way: "For whatsoever is not lawful to the whole church cannot by any ecclesiastical right become lawful to any of its members."[36] And in a similar vein Jankelevitch speaks of the subordination of the part to the whole:

Economy operates in accordance with temporal sequence, just as diplomacy operates in terms of coexistence. Just as the latter requires the sacrifice of the part for the whole, of

local interest for total interest, so the former, by its
temporal arrangements, decides on the sacrifice of the
present for the future, of the transitory moment to the
longest duration possible. Could you without absurdity
want to endanger, by pleasure of a moment, the superior
interests of a whole life?[37]

This subordination of the part to the whole is obvious if
the parts are homogeneous, but if the *presence* of the present
and actual gives it a superiority over the future, how is the
same subordination compelling?

Can we always claim that he who can do the most can do
the least? If this assertion expresses a formal truth, it would
be inconceivable that it could be opposed. We have an
excellent example of the contrary in the celebrated law that
was inspired by the great socialist leader Vandervelde and
adopted in Belgium after the First World War. This law
allowed the sale of two liters of alcohol to everyone,
although it forbade the sale of lesser amounts. However,
paradoxical, this law effectively contributed to combating
alcoholism among workers, which was its author's intent.

It is normal to consider species as subdivisions or parts of
a genus. From this, transposing reasoning concerning the
whole and its parts to reasoning that is relative to the genus
and the species requires only a small step. Most often, in this
type of argumentation, we do not seek to claim the
superiority of the genus over the species; rather, by reasoning about the species, we conclude to the genus or to a
species that is not yet examined: "anything that is to be
affirmed about the genus must be established for one of the
species; what does not belong to any species cannot belong
to the genus."[38]

This type of reasoning recalls the arguments by division to
which we have alluded. But whereas there is an already
existing agreement concerning species which constitute a
genus, the fact that a division can be freely created leads to

unexpected effects. For example:

> "You had good weather during your vacation?"
> "Oh yes; it rained only twice during the month."
> "Not more?"
> "No. First it rained for seven days, and then for three weeks."[39]

Argument by division, the use of which can serve not only as a means of proof but also as a means to create presence by the enumeration of the parts (see "amplification," p. 37), is the basis of the dilemma and of arguments *a pari* and *a contrario*.

In the dilemma, we examine two eventualities and conclude that both end in unpleasant consequences:

> And if anyone that professes himself to be a minister of the word of God, a preacher of the gospel of peace, teach otherwise, he either understands not, or neglects the business of his calling, and shall one day give an account thereof unto the Prince of Peace.[40]

Demosthenes reduced the choice of the Athenians with regard to Philip of Macedon to a dilemma:

> In a word, fellow Athenians, you must not lose sight of this fact: you have the choice between attacking Philip in his own land or being attacked by Philip in yours. Is it necessary to show the difference between making war in his land or in yours?[41]

The dilemma is constraining if we admit that the situation is reduced to one of the two stated alternatives. We are left with choosing the less destructive alternative. We might also observe that the presentation of a situation as a dilemma often tends to prove the bad faith of the opponent. Here is how Héron de Villefosse, "defender" of the authenticity of the tiara of Saitphernes, attacked an expert who opposed him:

> When M. Furtwangler discovers on some ancient monu-
> ment one of the figures or one of the motifs of the tiara, he
> declares for that reason that the tiara is a fraud; when he
> doesn't discover an example of the same motif or
> figures... he likewise concludes that the tiara is a fraud.
> This is a most extraordinary way of arguing.[42]

Not hampered by the nuances and not distinguishing all the
elements which would allow a person to conclude to the
falsity of the tiara, Héron de Villefosse, by reducing all
reasoning to a dilemma that leads to the same result, shows
the argumentation of his opponent to be the expression of a
preconceived point of view, entirely independent of the
results of a study of the tiara.

There are cases where presentation in the form of a
dilemma becomes inadmissible, because the two "horns"
lead to an absurdity. Sterne is very pleased when he can
make fun of one or another form of argumentation. We find
an amusing example in the reflections he attributes to the
lawyers of Strasbourg concerning a stranger's nose:

> Such a monstrous nose, said they, had it been a true nose,
> could not possibly have been suffered in civil society—
> and if false—to impose on society with such false signs
> and tokens, was still greater violation of its rights, and
> must have had still less mercy shown it.
>
> The only objection to this was, that if it proved any
> thing, it proved the stranger's nose was neither true nor
> false.[43]

In law, the relation between parts and the whole, between
species and the genus which contains them, gives rise to
arguments *a pari* and *a contrario*. Should we claim that what
holds for one species holds for the other, or should we
contrast them? When a rule of law declares that sons inherit
from their parents, does the law hold equally for daughters,
or does it deny them a share in the inheritance? Only the

context provides the correct interpretation. The history of law contains instances in which a rule has received one interpretation when at its passage another was intended. The fact that a person can waver between these two types of arguments clearly brings out the distinction between argumentation and formal demonstration. The application of the argumentative scheme presupposes a decision concerning the weight, in a given situation, of the reasons presented in favor of either the assimilation or differentiation of the two species of the same genus.

5. Weights and Measures, and Probabilities

Comparison constitutes a quasi-logical argument when it does not give rise to a real weighing and measuring that uses a system of weights and measures. Nevertheless, the persuasive effect of such comparisons derives from the underlying idea that the person making the comparison can if necessary support his judgment through a process of verification. In saying that "her cheeks are as red as apples" or that "he is richer than Croesus," he seems to express an opinion that can be checked.

When Cicero affirmed, "It is the same crime, whether it is stealing from the state or giving bribes contrary to public interest,"[44] he gave the same weight to an action which does not fall under the law as he did to a punishable crime.

Although in the actual process of weighing and measuring the standard is neutral and invariable, comparisons of all types are colored by the influence of the chosen comparative term, because the two are, by the very comparison, conjoined in the same class and become thereby more or less homogeneous. To say of a writer that he is inferior to one of greater renown, or that he is superior to a nonentity, is in each instance to express a defensible judgment; yet the import of each comparison is quite different. In bringing together two widely separated terms, the inferior term is elevated and the superior term somewhat lowered. This idea did not escape Bossuet, who emphasized:

> Pious sovereigns are willing that all their glory disappear before that of God; and, far from being saddened that their power is thereby diminished, they know that they are never more profoundly revered than when they are humbled by comparisons with God.[45]

Here we see the superiority of the incomparable—what can only be compared to itself, what can truly be considered unique.

Plotinus, having shown the superiority of the One over all other reality, yet fearing its devaluation said:

> We cannot think of the First as moving towards any other; He holds his own manner of being before any other was; even Being we withhold and therefore all relation to beings.[46]

In a similar way, La Bruyère, speaking of the value of great artists, wrote: "V— is a painter, C— a musician, and the author of Pyramus is a poet; but Mignard is Mignard, Lulli is Lulli, and Corneille is Corneille."[47]

The comparison, in bringing different actions together, places them at a certain level which the interlocutors mutually accept. But revealing a divergence in this respect never fails to produce a comic effect. A pretty girl and an old, ill-tempered woman are waiting for a bus; the old woman indignantly refuses a cigarette.

> "Smoke on the street? I'd rather kiss the first man who comes along."
> "So would I, but while we are waiting, why not light up?"[48]

In quasi-logical argumentation it is rare that the term of comparison is determined in a compelling way. Since recourse to this argument aims less to inform than to impress, the indication of an absolute numerical magnitude can be less effective than the indication of a relative magnitude, but only on the condition that the term of comparison be well chosen. In underscoring the immensity of a country to a native of France, it would be more advantageous, for example, to describe a country as nine times larger than France than half as large as Brazil.

The term of comparison can be used as a foil. Thus enthusiastic descriptions of a Golden Age or of the "good old days" are used to depreciate the age or country in which one lives.

Often the comparison derives from a sacrifice: the latter measures the value people attribute to what they want to get or hold. Hence the importance of martyrs as guarantors of the faith. "I believe," writes Pascal, "only the histories, whose witnesses got themselves killed."[49] A statement by Calvin corresponds to this. Contrasting the Catholics' weak attachment to their religion to the determination of the Protestants, he writes: "Quite the opposite is our assurance, which fears neither the terror of death nor even God's judgment seat."[50]

Plotinus does not hesitate to use the argument that ascetic denial proves the value of the mystic state: "All that she [the soul] had welcomed of old—office, power, wealth, beauty, knowledge—of all that she tells her scorn as she never could had she not found their better."[51]

Believers can be humble and without renown; their numbers make up for their lack of prestige, as in the Legend of the 11,000 virgins who accompanied St. Ursula.

In the argument by sacrifice, in the absence of an objective standard, things are judged only by the value people attach to them. Is this value a constant? Nothing indicates it is. The sacrificed good can become an object of ambivalence, as can a long-sought goal:

Too high a degree of suffering in relation to what the heart prompts can produce one or another of two attitudes: either the violent rejection of the object to which too much has been sacrificed, or else a clinging to it in a sort of despair.[52]

Useless sacrifice represents a devaluation of the person who made it. Soldiers who had fallen in an unsuccessful offensive were in one instance called by their comrades "those who must start all over again."[53]

The argument by sacrifice becomes comic if it deals with something which does not appeal to the self-interest of the interlocutor. "An employer, questioning a candidate for a position, is surprised: 'You ask for a very high salary and have so little experience.' ['Yes,' the candidate replies.] 'The work is so much more difficult when you don't know how to handle it.' "[54]

We can add to quasi-logical or quasi-mathematical arguments all those which refer to noncalculable probabilities, or at least to ideas that underlie the calculus of probabilities. Here are two lines of reasoning based on the idea that the probability of a better choice is increased as the number of solutions between which it is necessary to choose is increased. Isocrates advises the admission of young people to deliberative assemblies:

Since the quality of our judgments does not depend on our age but on our temperament and our diligence, why not make it obligatory to call on the experience of two generations in order to make possible the choice of the wisest counsel on all matters?[55]

This is also the argument Locke used in opposing the tyranny of princes in religious matters:

For there being but one truth, one way to Heaven, what hope is there that more men would be led into it if they had no rule but the religion of the court and were put under the necessity to quit the light of their own reason? ...The narrow way would be much straightened.... One country alone would be in the right.[56]

In both cases the authors claim to prefer the arrangements that offer the greater number of options. The problem of participation in deliberative assemblies, as well as that of religious liberty, is reduced to one of its aspects alone, that is, to the greater or lesser probability of reaching the desired result.

Considering our life to be a limited wager in comparison to eternal salvation, to the infinity of the eternal happy life to be gained, Pascal invites us to play because the chances are in our favor:

> ...every player stakes a certainty to gain an uncertainty, and yet he stakes a finite certainty to gain a finite uncertainty, without transgressing against reason. There is not an infinite distance between the certainty staked and the uncertainty of the gain; that is untrue. In truth, there is an infinity between the certainty of gain and the certainty of loss. But the uncertainty of the gain is proportioned to the certainty of the stake according to the proportion of the chances of gain and loss. Hence it comes that, if there are as many risks on one side as on the other, the course is to play even; and then the certainty of the stake is equal to the uncertainty of the gain, so far is it from fact that there is an infinite distance between them. And so our proposition is of infinite force, when there is the finite to stake in a game where there are equal risks of gain and of loss, and the infinite to gain.[57]

Leibniz and Bentham wished to apply probabilities to the appraisal of the value of proofs and testimonies; similarly, in their casuistry, the Jesuits had recourse to probabilism. All these techniques presuppose the reduction of a problem to only one of its aspects, noncalculable but capable of evaluation in terms of its frequency. But this reduction can lead to the disregard of other possibly essential aspects. Pascal emphasized this point in the *Provincial Letters*. Because of the difficulty of this reduction of a problem to formal and quantitative aspects, it is rare that quasi-logical arguments can themselves carry conviction. They must be supplemented by arguments based on the structure of reality.

8. Arguments Based on the Structure of Reality

As SOON AS elements of reality are associated with each other in a recognized liaison, it is possible to use this liaison as the basis for an argumentation which allows us to pass from what is accepted to what we wish to have accepted.

We have seen how Bossuet, arguing from the bond, traditional in the Church, between the altar and the pulpit, tried to obtain from the believers the same respect for God's word that he assigned to the body of Christ in the Eucharist.

Generally, the structures that are appealed to are of another kind. Most arguments that are based on reality appeal to liaisons of succession,[1] such as cause to effect, or liaisons of coexistence,[2] such as the relation between the person and his acts. These are two different ways of structuring reality. In liaisons of succession, phenomena of the same level are placed in relationship, while in liaisons of coexistence, argumentation is based on terms that represent things that belong to unequal levels, such as an essence and its manifestations.

1. Liaisons of Succession

Starting from the affirmation of a causal tie between phenomena, argumentation can be directed toward the search for causes, the determination of effects, and the evaluation of a fact by its consequences. In intentional acts, determining the cause goes with determining the motive for the action. The purpose of the argumentation that is developed is to account for a phenomenon, to explain it, and at times to direct further inquiries. The discovery of a corpse raises a series of questions. Was the death natural or the result of a crime? If the latter, what could have provoked it? Who had an interest in killing the victim? Among the suspects, who had the desire and the opportunity to do it? Are the presuppositions at one's disposal precise and coherent? To what degree do they explain the course of events? Would other hypotheses not be just as acceptable?

It should be noted that the same type of reasoning serves equally well in private deliberation and in argumentation with other people. The latter will be effective only if there is agreement between interlocutors on the possible motives of an action, their pertinence, and their probability in a given context. The person who wins too often in a game of chance is suspected of cheating because only in this way can his success be comprehensible to us. If several testimonies agree, although the witnesses have not been previously coordinated, we are led to conclude that they witnessed the same event, the reality of which they attest.

Having accepted the existence of correlations, natural laws, or the principle that the same causes produce the same effects, one is able to construct hypotheses within a given context and verify them with the appropriate inquiries.

The *pragmatic argument*[3] permits us to appraise a fact through its consequences. For Bentham, it is the only valid argumentation when it is a question of adopting a norm:

> What is it to offer a *good reason* with respect to a law? It is to allege the good or evil which the law tends to produce. ... What is it to offer a *false reason?* It is the alleging for or against a law something else than its good or evil effects.[4]

The argument from consequences seems to be so obvious as to need no justification. Consequences can be observed or foreseen, ascertained or presumed. And pragmatic reasoning allows for even the justification of superstitious behavior, as in this example:

> If there are thirteen at a table—if I light three cigarettes on one match—well, I'm worried and can't concentrate. However, if I insist on only twelve, or refuse to light the third cigarette, then I feel reassured and I can think clearly again. Therefore these demands are legitimate and reasonable. They are logical and I am logical with myself.[5]

The pragmatic argument, which seems to reduce the value of a cause to that of its consequences, gives the impression that all values are of the same order. It is thus that the truth of an idea can, in pragmatism, only be judged by its effects, the failure of an enterprise or life likewise serving as a criterion of its irrationality or inauthenticity.

Max Scheler described as pharisaic the notion that identifies the moral with the useful.[6] Again, Simone Weil rebelled against the arguments in favor of Christianity that resemble pharmaceutical publicity of the "before and after" sort; they seemed to say, "Look what a miserable lot men were before Christ."[7]

Yet the gravest objections against the pragmatic argument derive from the difficulties of its application. How do we determine the indefinite chain of consequences that result from an action, and how are we to impute to a single cause the consequences that result most often from the concurrence of several events?

This problem is illustrated by the various difficulties which were brought about by the application of Article 1382 of the French Civil Code: "Any act whatsoever of the person who inflicts injury on another obligates the one through whose fault it occurred to make reparation." What conse-

quences are to be imputed to the wrongful act? To what
degree should it be considered the sole cause of the events
which follow in the chain of cause and effect?

For example, Eve's sinful act incited Adam to disobey
God and thereby deprived them both of Paradise and
immortality—but it also resulted in giving birth to the whole
human race. When, as in this example, an event is thought to
have various, and even opposite consequences, is it good or
evil? It is to answer this objection that the utilitarian calculus
was invented; this calculus aims to reduce the sum total of an
action's consequences to a positive or negative quantitative
result. The criticisms that have been set forth against
utilitarianism would also tell against use of the pragmatic
argument if this argument (1) claimed in every case to be
able to reduce the complete cluster of consequences to an
objectively calculable result and moreover (2) disallowed
recourse to arguments of any other kind. But this double
claim is that of Bentham's utilitarianism and not neccess-
sarily that of every use of the pragmatic argument, for the
pragmatic argument would claim to be an important one,
but certainly not the only one admissable in a controversy.

The best proof that Bentham's double claim does not
always apply to the pragmatic argument is the fact that the
same causal chain will be evaluated differently depending on
whether it is considered as a succession of causes and effects
or, if an intentional element intervenes, as the relation of a
means to an end. The very fact that an event can be
interpreted in one or another way can give rise to the effects
of style, such as *antithesis,* used by Cicero to oppose the
consequences of an action to the end of that action: "Your
iniquity has not inflicted a miserable exile on me, but has
prepared a glorious return instead."[8]

The opposition between consequences and ends has at
times an unexpected and even comic result: "A rich heir paid
his servants handsomely to cut dignified figures at the

funeral of his father. But the rascals, the more they were paid to look sad, the happier they became."[9] The consequences can be diametrically opposed to the desired end, especially when the activities of many individuals are not coordinated. Thus Anatole France began his *Thaïs* with this striking formulation: "At that time the desert was peopled by anchorites."[10]

We should note that certain facts produce the desired consequences only if they are *not* perceived as means to an end, as devices. A passage from Proust illustrates this point:

> ... If a man were to regret that he was not sufficiently courted in society, I should not advise him to pay more calls, to keep an even finer carriage, I should tell him not to accept any invitation, to live shut up in his room, to admit nobody, and that then there would be a queue outside his door. Or rather I should not tell him so. For it is a certain road to success which succeeds only like the road to love, that is to say if one has not adopted it with that object in view, if, for instance, you confine yourself to your room because you are seriously ill, or are supposed to be, or are keeping a mistress shut up with you whom you prefer to society (or for all these reasons at once), this will justify another person, who is not aware of the woman's existence, and simply because you decline to see him, in preferring you to all the people who offer themselves, and attaching himself to you.[11]

Similarly, rhetorical effects, when they do not seem to correspond to a sincere feeling, when they do not appear natural, are written off as "devices." Their use would surely lead people to view rhetoric in a bad light.

Means have only a relative value because they depend on the value accorded the end, which is considered to be independent. Yet it happens that means are transformed into ends, as in the case of avarice or of love:

One loves already when one senses in the loved one a
source of inexhaustible, vague, unknown happiness....
Then the loved one is still a means—a means that is
unique and impossible to replace, by countless, vague
ends.... One really loves, one loves one's friend *for
himself,* as the miser loves his gold, when, the end having
ceased to be considered, the means have become the end,
and the value of the beloved has ceased to be relative and
has become absolute.[12]

The transformation of a means into an end, and of an end
into a means, coincides with its valuation or devaluation.
Although courage is indispensable for victory in war,
Isocrates makes war an indispensable means for the realization of courage: "In my view it is some god who has brought
about this war out of admiration for [the warriors'] courage,
in order to prevent them from being unrecognized and
ending their lives in obscurity."[13] Seeing war as only a means
by which to show the courage of men seems to verge on the
ridiculous. The comic comes forth in the advertising of
certain undertakers, inspired by the advertisements for
photographic equipment ("Push this button and we do the
rest"): "Simply die and we do the rest."[14] Beyond a certain
limit, an argumentative device no longer persuades but
provokes laughter.

Where is this limit? The disproportion between values
considered as means and as ends must be such that we
cannot take seriously suggestions made ironically, such as
Swift's recommendation sanctioning an infallible means by
which the children of the Irish poor would be no burden to
their parents and country: he recommended roasting them
in order to provide supplementary nourishment for adults.
After the horrible experiences of World War II, this
suggestion was read to school children and was no longer
thought comical but frightful.[15]

In an old film, a prostitute wanted to change her ways and

marry a man who ran a cartage business. Her pimp asked the drayman: "How would you treat someone who stole one of your wagons? You should expect the same kind of treatment from a person whose meal ticket you have taken away." The transformation of a human being into a mere means provokes laughter or indignation, depending on the situation. But in some contexts it may seem quite normal.

The means/end relation is fundamental to the arguments of *waste,* of *redundancy,* and of *the decisive.*

The existence of an effective means allows us to realize a desire and gives the desire a stability sufficient to transform it into an end. Bossuet invites sinners to repentance by emphasizing the fact that God, in his mercy, provides them with the means of salvation. Jesus' sacrifice has made it possible for the faithful to do penance for their sins. Their impenitence deepens the sorrow of the Virgin by making her Son's sacrifice useless: instead of providing a means of salvation, his death seems a waste. This is a form of reasoning Bossuet used frequently in his sermons.[16]

To avoid wasting effort in attaining a certain end, a person will continue a project until it is completed. This argument will serve equally well to motivate those who have remarkable gifts, exceptional learning, or skill, and do not want to neglect them.

What is redundant is by that very fact devalued; what is decisive gains in importance. "The action, which, under the circumstances, can attain its full bearing and should thus not be considered a waste, will thereby gain in value and this militates in favor of its being done."[17]

When the gap between the theses the audience accepts and those the speaker defends is too great to be overcome all at once, it is advisable to divide the difficulty and arrive at the same result gradually. Instead of going from A to D, one offers to lead the interlocutor first to B, then to C, and finally to D. This is the method or device of stages.

To forestall this technique, the opponent will use the *argument of direction,* which, foreseeing or anticipating future developments, opposes the first step, fearing that it will lead to a "slippery slope" that will allow no stopping and end in total capitulation.

This dynamic conception of argumentation introduces a new ambiguity into the process. Will the one arguing for the passage from A to B be satisfied with the change this brings about, or will he consider it only as a stage in a certain direction? We should note, in this regard, that the proposed change can lead, not to an easier passage to C and then D, but to the generalization of the passage from A to B by the technique of precedent. In fact, because of this technique, any resolution can be considered a precedent which would facilitate, in the future, the passage from A to B. Set against this technique is the fear of precedent, which, like the argument of direction, resists the adoption of a solution that would be welcomed if exceptional but is unacceptable as a generalization.

Henceforth, discussion can center upon the import of a resolution: the possibility of stopping at the appointed stage or of considering the measure as a development that is in a case by itself.

When a speaker proposes the immediate passage from A to D, his opponent can suggest a compromise, the passage to B, presenting this measure as a stage in a gradual progress, in the hope that it will not be necessary to continue, or, in any case, in the certainty that time will be gained before having to accept the undesirable measure. Bentham calls this the "snail's-pace argument" and classifies it among the "fallacies of delay."[18] But this procedure is no more fallacious than other argumentative techniques. It consists in "throwing over the ballast," that is, in accepting inevitable sacrifices when one is not in a position to do otherwise. In this case, it is the person who wants to obtain everything at once who insists that when his opponent argues for *gradual* progress he is "making out of a mere word an excuse for leaving undone an indefinite multitude of things, which the arguer is convinced, and cannot forbear acknowledging, ought to be done."[19]

The opposition between quantitative and qualitative change corresponds to this technique of division. At what moment does change become no longer one of degree but one of nature? At what point does taxation become confiscation? At what moment does the nationalization of entire branches of industry transform the economy of a country into a socialist one? This discussion is only a variant of the method of stages, wherein each stage is of a quantitative nature, but the end result may become qualitative change, a change of nature.

The argument of unlimited development looks to only one value; that value is not limited by any other that could be an obstacle to its own inordinate development. It professes to consider each realization in the given field only as a stage in an indefinite progression. But it goes without saying that the believer in a pluralism of values will counter that any value, pushed to the limit, leads to incompatibilities with other values whose realization it impedes. Infinite liberty is as incompatible with reality as with the coexistence of several liberties.

The idea of unlimited development, indicating a direction of thought, can serve, in its exaggeration, as *hyperbole* as well as *litotes*.[20]

2. Liaisons of Coexistence

While liaisons of succession join elements of the same nature, such as events and phenomena which are linked by a causal connection, the liaisons of coexistence establish a tie between realities on unequal levels; one is shown to be the expression or manifestation of the other. Such are the relations between a person and his actions, his attitudes, and his works. Although philosophically and in an abstract way, the liaison of coexistence is symbolized by the relation between act and essence, it seems that the prototype of such a liaison is the relationship between a person and his manifestations. Everything that is affirmed about a person is justified by how that person manifests himself, but it is the unity and stability of the person that unifies the totality of his acts. It is the person's character, the intentions attributed to him, that give meaning and an explanatory import to his behavior.

If the person is formed from his manifestations, the latter are interpreted in terms of the idea people get of the person. The person and his acts are in constant interaction, and it is difficult to say which element precedes the other. In the liaisons of succession, cause always precedes effect; but we know that philosophically the relation between a person and his acts can be explained in two dramatically opposing ways. While for Leibniz the monad is given all at once and its existence flows out in time in a way determined by its nature, Existentialism holds that "existence precedes essence" and that therefore the person *is* nothing but a function of his acts. The theory of argumentation need not take a position in an ontological debate. It is enough to state that the idea one develops of the person and the manner of comprehending his acts are in constant interaction.

Everything that is connected to the structure of the person will be considered as essential and endowed with a stability that is denied to what is only accidental and transitory. "Any argument about the person has to do with his stability: it is assumed when an act is interpreted as a function of the person, and it is failure to respect this stability which is deplored when someone is reproached for incoherence or unjustified change."[21]

The formation of the person affords him a certain continuity. The person is considered responsible for his past actions, which contribute to his reputation, to his merit or demerit. It is the person who is praised or blamed, compensated or chastised.

Social techniques, language, morality, law, and religion help accentuate this impression of unity and stability, but the most remarkable of these techniques is the attribution of a proper name. A timeless qualification, the epithet (e.g., Richard the Lionhearted), stresses this immutable aspect of personality and its freedom from contingencies. Kenneth Burke, the American critic who has best analyzed the argumentative usage of literary techniques, has underscored this trait:

> A hero is first of all a man who does heroic things: and his "heroism" resides in his acts. But next, a hero can be a man with the potentialities of heroic action. Soldiers on the way to the wars are heroes in this sense ... Or a man may be considered a hero because he *has done* heroic acts, whereas in his present state as a hero he may be too old or weak to do such acts at all.[22]

But besides this stability, which solidifies the person, people stress the person's freedom, spontaneity, capacity for change, adaptation, and even conversion. By this the person differentiates himself from an object. Existentialism goes as far as to deny the person an essence, a nature; this would be settled only at his death.

And yet, from the standpoint of argumentation, the person is the author of his acts, an enduring being around which and in relation to which all things considered as his manifestations can be grouped.

It is this ambiguous image of the person, and moreover of all the liaisons of coexistence constructed on this model, that gives the human sciences their specific character, insofar as they are thought of as sciences of mind as opposed to nature. It is above all in law and in ethics that the act-person liaison, together with its correlative notions of responsibility, imputability, freedom, and constraint, plays a characteristic role.[23]

How do acts influence our conception of the person? The person can withstand the repercussions of any new act, for we grant to him a freedom, a capacity for change. The more a person is sunk into history, the more rigid the image we have of him becomes. But this rigidity is always relative; it is subject to a change of perspective that will grant more importance, for the structuring of the person, to certain previously disregarded acts, the decisive character of which is now emphasized. Since persons are known only through their manifestations (except in the case of persons such as God or Satan, whose natures are given a priori), our humanistic conception of right prevents us from punishing people preventively, before they have committed a crime. The freedom granted them prohibits us from comparing them to a harmful animal, a poisonous snake or rabid dog. Every act is considered less the mark of an unalterable nature than a contribution to the building of the person which comes to an end only in death.

A judgment about the person of others at times reflects back upon the one who passes it. Someone who wrongly accuses another of thoughtlessness or partiality can be charged with these in turn. In the case of value judgments based upon a frequently disputed interpretation, every judgment can, in the absence of indisputable criteria, be turned against the person who expressed it. In the story of the Emperor's New Clothes, the tailor convinced the king that the clothing he would give him could be seen only by people with impeccable moral qualities. No courtier dared say aloud what he saw, fearing to reveal his own immorality.

The tailor's deceit was shown up by a naive child who asked why the king was naked. The unquestioned innocence of the child did away with the relationship established by the tailor between what was seen and the morality of the viewer. This tale, which sets up an interaction between the subject's character and perceptions, pushes to the limit the frequently accepted interaction between the subject and his value judgments and throws suspicion on every assertion which cannot be verified.

Past acts contribute to the good or bad reputation of the agent. The good name a person enjoys becomes a form of capital embodied in his person, an asset it is legitimate to use in case of need. Moreover, it creates a favorable or unfavorable disposition on the part of others, because it is in the context formed by the person that people interpret all his acts, attributing to him an *intention* that conforms to the idea they have of him.

This phenomenon of interpretation allowed the American psychologist S.E. Asch to criticize the methods of his colleagues, who had ascertained that the same proposition was judged in a favorable or unfavorable way depending on whether it was attributed to one author or another. They saw in this the influence of prestige, which they considered irrational. Asch showed that this was not the case—that the statement was interpreted differently according to the context provided by the person of its author.[24]

The most striking case of divergent interpretations concerns the activity of persons, such as God and Satan, whose conduct is judged in advance as favorable or unfavorable. Although they both contributed to bringing all kinds of afflictions down upon Job, Calvin assures us that God acted well and Satan damnably because their intentions were diametrically opposed.[25]

It is the intention, which is hidden behind the acts, which becomes essential; it is this which must be sought behind the exterior manifestations of the person, for it is this which gives them their significance and bearing. Hence a double judgment, one concerning the act itself and the other the agent. "We speak," writes Lalande, "of intelligent errors, and not without reason: Descartes is full of them; of honorable crimes or misdemeanors, like Saint Vincent de Paul cheating for the poor."[26]

The influence of the person on the manner in which his acts are received is exercised through the medium of *prestige,* which is the quality that leads others to imitate his acts.[27] "The example of the great," writes Gracian, "is a rhetorician of such power that it can persuade people to commit the most infamous acts."[28] People imitate his behavior and adopt his opinions. From this comes the importance of the *argument from authority,* where the prestige of a person or a group is used to gain acceptance of a thesis.

The argument from authority—*argumentum ad vericundiam*—was attacked most violently in scientific circles, because it was widely and improperly used to combat any novelty, discovery, or change which might have challenged those authorities traditionally considered infallible. It is clear that no authority can prevail against a demonstrable truth, but this is not true in the case of opinions or value judgments. Besides, in a controversy it is most often not the *argument* from authority which is questioned but the *authority* who is called upon. Pascal, who mocks "people of influence," does not hesitate to invoke St. Augustine, and Calvin rejects the Church's authority but accepts that of the prophets.

The authorities invoked vary considerably. Sometimes, the authority will be "unanimous opinion" or "general opinion." Sometimes it will be certain categories of men such as "scientists," "philosophers," the "Fathers of the Church," the "prophets." At other times, the authority will be impersonal: "physics," "doctrine," "religion," or the "Bible." And yet at other times, the authorities will be especially designated by name."[29]

The argument from authority is of interest only in the absence of demonstrable proof. It comes to the support of other arguments, and the person who uses it will not fail to accord value to the authority which agrees with his thesis, while depreciating the authority which sustains that of his opponent. Ultimately, the only indisputable authority is divine authority. This is the basic argument justifying submission to the words of Jesus:

> A master [Jesus] who enjoys such great authority, even though his doctrine may be obscure, deserves to have his words believed, *ipsum audite....* Do not let us search for the reasons for the truths he teaches us: the whole reason is that he has spoken.[30]

Except for the case of an absolute authority, the conflict of authorities requires a criterion by which a settlement is brought about. Today, "competence" is the most commonly advanced criterion, but there are others, such as tradition, antiquity, universality. The search for a new criterion most often accompanies the rejection of already established authorities.

A curious use of the argument from authority occurs when the qualified authority cannot understand an assertion. When this happens, people tend to conclude that the assertion is incomprehensible, that no one can understand it.

To avoid conflicts of competence, law has made "competence" a technical notion. That judge is competent to judge a litigation who has been appointed in accordance with the rules of procedure. He decides with authority, and the authority of the judgment can be likened to the truth before which everyone must bow.

The interaction of the person and his acts, which is normal
in all argumentation, can be either arrested or curbed. In
certain cases the influence of the person on the act will be set
aside; in others, that of the act upon the person.

When a person uses a method to prove a truth, to establish
a fact in an incontestable way, the character of the person
who affirms the fact does not in any way modify the status of
the affirmation. That a criminal discovered a formula for a
poison does not cause us to doubt the strength of the
preparation. (On the contrary, "an error of fact drowns a
wise man in ridicule." The interaction of person on act is
replaced by an action which goes from the act to the person.)

To obtain the reverse effect, to protect the person, it
would be necessary to consider him divine or perfect. Whatever God does or says must be interpreted in terms of his
perfection, to which nothing could be opposed. Leibniz
underscores this in his *Theodicy:*

> I have indicated already that the things which can be
> opposed to the goodness and justice of God are only
> appearances, which would have weight against a man, but
> which are naught when applied to God and when weighed
> against the demonstrations which assure us of the infinite
> perfection of his attributes. [31]

The techniques indicated, which in one sense or another
prevent interaction, can be called *techniques of severance.*
They rarely have occasion to appear in argumentation.
More frequently used are *techniques of restraint,* which aim
not to arrest but to curb the import of an act, its influence
upon the image of the person.

This is the role or predispositions or preconceptions,
favorable or unfavorable, in maintaining, insofar as it is
possible, the opinion one person has of another in the face of
acts which at first sight seem to contradict it. The one will
interpret the other's act in conformity with the preconcep-

tion so as to preserve a harmony between the act, thus interpreted, and the conception of the other person he has already developed. If the dissonance between the two is too obvious, he will make use of other techniques of restraint in order to prevent too great a reverberation of the act upon the agent. He will consider as negligible those acts that happened too far back in time, in childhood or adolescence; or those that arise from special circumstances; or those that are exceptional, because they were committed in a state of drunkenness or in the grip of intense emotion. He will place responsibility on social surroundings, poor education, bad company.

When it is the act or opinion that a person wants to shelter from the idea he has of someone, he will attribute that act or opinion to another source. Bossuet, in his desire to have the sermons of corrupt preachers listened to with respect, borrowed an analogy from St. Augustine:

> The shrub bears fruit that does not belong to it but is no less the fruit of the vine though the shrub supports it. . . . Do not scorn this grape on the excuse that you see it among the thorns; do not reject this doctrine because it is surrounded by bad morals; it still comes from God.[32]

On the other hand, someone who wants to attack another's testimony or value judgment will try to do just the opposite and establish a bond between the agent and his acts by disqualifying the person from whom they come. In his *Rhetoric* Aristotle writes that one may "return calumny for calumny and say 'It is monstrous to trust the man's statements when you cannot trust the man himself'."[33] The attack *ad personam* had been recommended by the theoreticians of antiquity. Today, except when it is a matter of disqualifying a delinquent witness, this device is looked upon unfavorably. In any case, in matters where the techniques of severance allow the separation of the speaker from his discourse, it is offensive—and ineffective—to attack the speaker rather than the thesis he is defending.

When it is a question not of facts but of opinions, and especially of value judgments, not only the person of the speaker but also the function he exercises, the role he assumes, undeniably influences the way the audience will receive his words. The same remarks, spoken by the defending attorney, the prosecutor, or the judge, will be received and understood in very different ways. But, inversely, the speaker's words create an image of him the importance of which ought not be underestimated. Aristotle considers this, under the name of *oratorical ethos,* as one of the three components of effectiveness in persuasion, the two others being *logos* and *pathos*—respectively, the appeal to reason through argumentation and the rhetorical procedures which aim at arousing the audience's passions.[34]

Based on the model of the act-person liaison, other liaisons of coexistence are developed, the use of which is typical of the human sciences. When the historical sciences shift their focus of interest from individuals to peoples, eras, institutions, and political and economic regimes, they lay stress on new categories, formed in imitation of the person. As the person is manifested through his acts, so also are national groups manifested as entities through their members. Thus one can speak of the *Volksgeist.* But on the other hand, besides the idea people have of a group, the favorable or unfavorable preconception they have of it also influences the attitude they adopt toward those who make it up.

But the individual-group liaison presents problems *sui generis* which stem from the fact that the individual is normally a member of several groups. It is often difficult to say, without hesitation, which one the person truly identifies with or represents. This problem never arises concerning the liaison established between a person and his acts.

A member of a minority group is more easily considered representative than is a member of a majority: a black lost in a white population, a white among blacks, a foreigner among a mass of people native to a region all more readily allow for a generalization to be made from them. It would be ridiculous to consider every indigenous person as representative of the majority; on the contrary, he would be more readily considered by his compatriots as representative of a regional, professional, or confessional subgroup.

People are members of certain groups from birth and for the duration of their lives, according to the race or people into which they are born. They enter other groups, professional or political, at a specific time and can withdraw from them. Certain groups are recognized and protected by institutions, law, customs, and tradition. Others, such as groups of friends in a class or in sports, are formed spontaneously and later dissolve. Cultures, religions, and ideologies contribute to the bonds of solidarity among a group's members, bonds which are accentuated through conflict with other groups, especially in periods of national or civil war.

Certain individuals, in terms of their function, are considered representative: a foreign ambassador, the head of a church, the president of a party are designated institutional spokesmen. But to what degree are other members of a group representative of it? Normally, the action of each member will influence the opinion that outsiders form of the group. To break this bond, the techniques of severance and restraint have been instituted. When it is a question of "severing" a member, or of his official condemnation, the severance of the liaison needs to be most manifest when this member could be considered most representative.

Liaisons of coexistence also establish a connection between events, individuals, works, and the historical period from which they arise. We speak of the medieval or Renaissance man, describing an ideal type. It is true that one must admit exceptions, precursors or throwbacks who are linked to a period before or after the one in which they actually lived. It must be readily admitted that efforts to systematize and explain a complex and multiple reality cannot be achieved without including exceptions which appear to be secondary in relation to the total picture.

On the same model, one can treat literary or artistic movements (romanticism), styles (the baroque), economic or legal structures (capitalism, feudalism), ideologies (liberalism, socialism)—all the categories which history cannot do without.[35] The manner in which these categories are developed—these "ideal types," as Max Weber called them—and the connections they maintain with experience, with the "sources" of history, determine most of the methodological problems of the human sciences. Studies on the periodization of history offer many examples.

Let us not forget that the categories developed in the humanities do not have the fixity and stability of objects and are not guaranteed by biological relationships as in the animal species; rather, they are constructions of the mind, tied to a distinction between what is essential and what is accessory, accidental, or negligible. The most general liaison of coexistence is the connection between essence and the acts which are its manifestations. The effort of metaphysicians to explain by a comon essence what individuals have in common, and through the intervention of external elements such as matter and accident, what diversifies them, can be brought together within the class of all the argumentative techniques that are used in the liaisons of coexistence.

It is in relation to essence that we can understand the contrast between use and abuse. "Abuse" designates those activities or actions which should not be included in one's idea of the way something normally works. Through the technique of severance, the essence of a thing can be kept sheltered from what is abusive. Similarly, the ideas of "too little" or "too much" are defined explicitly or implicitly in relation to essence.

An essence may be linked to a person through the use of such rhetorical figures as *personification, apostrophe,* and *prosopopoeia.*

3. Symbolic Liaisons, Double Hierarchies, Differences of Order

Symbolic liaisons can be included among the liaisons of coexistence; these exist between the symbol and what it evokes and are characterized by the relation of *participation.* They are set in a mythic or speculative vision of a whole in which symbol and thing symbolized are equally parts. In such a vision, realities which are separated in time can nonetheless be coexistent in a nontemporal conception of history. Thus Adam is thought of as a prefiguration of Christ, not in a relationship of causality, but in a relationship of participation which is at the core of a divine plan which establishes their solidarity.

Because of this relationship of participation, doing something to the symbol directly affects that which is symbolized. To spit on the flag is to scoff at the country symbolized by it; to brandish the cross is to be a spokesman for a militant Christianity. A person insults a religion by attacking its cultic objects. The symbol is indispensable for arousing fervor, religious or patriotic, because emotions can rarely be attached to purely abstract ideas.

In a romantic conception of the world in which nature seems to participate in the life of man, events which touch human life are "reflected" in the heavens. Nothing is more characteristic in this respect than the "tragic heaven" which forms the background of a good number of paintings representing Jesus' crucifixion. Let us note that because of the irrational character of the majority of stories which show symbolic liaisons, techniques of severance and restraint hardly apply.

It is only when a symbolic liaison has become institutionalized that argumentation can play a role. If the king is the symbol of the state, he ceases to perform this role after his abdication. It nonetheless happens that someone may be chosen as a symbol not because he embodies what is best in the country, as does a Nobel Prize winner or boxing champion, but because there is no distinctive, individualized sign which distinguishes him from the people, as is the case with the unknown soldier. Nevertheless, the homage of everyone who wants to honor both the nation and all those who sacrificed themselves for its preservation can be focused upon the latter.

It is insofar as a symbol gives presence to what is symbolized that it can serve as a figure of rhetoric, such as *metonymy.*

Double hierarchy arguments, based on liaisons either of succession or of coexistence, can be classed among the arguments based on the structure of reality. The argument *a fortiori* is one application of a double hierarchy.

A double hierarchy that is purely quantitative can be based on a statistical correlation, as in a line of reasoning that infers from the fact that one man is taller than another to the fact that his limbs are longer. But most interesting are the qualitative double hierarchies, for example, the conclusion from the superiority of an end to the superiority of the means which allows one to realize it.[36] On the superiority of men to birds is based the argument *a fortiori* according to which "God, inasmuch as he cares for the sparrows, will not neglect reasonable beings, who are infinitely more dear to him."[37]

The most frequent double hierarchy arguments are based on liaisons of coexistence and specifically on the connection between a person and his acts. Aristotle expresses this idea very clearly: "The attribute is more desirable which belongs to the better and more honorable subject, e.g., to a god rather than to a man, and to the soul rather than to the body."[38]

Thus divine laws are superior to human laws,[39] and true knowledge, which nourishes the mind of a god, is superior to "the food of semblance" which is the food of fallen souls.[40] If there is indeed a hierarchy of beings, one might try to make a hierarchy of forms of conduct correspond to it. Plotinus believed that the mandatory rule for conducting oneself is to approach the One and stand away from sensible objects, which are lowest of all.[41] Ontology would thus serve as the basis for a hierarchy of forms of conduct. From the superiority of people over animals, of adults over children, we easily draw moral lessons: "Don't behave like a pig or wild animal—act like a grown-up," we often say to children.

It is clear that the usefulness of this argument presupposes agreement on the hierarchy from which one starts. It is only in a society which possesses an aristocratic vision of itself that the conduct of the nobles will be noble and that of the villains, that is, inhabitants of the countryside, villainous.

To end this examination of arguments based on the structure of reality, it would be useful to point out the importance attached to differences of nature or order in comparison with simple differences of degree.

The introduction of considerations relative to order, whether they result from the opposition of a difference of degree to a difference of nature, or from that of a difference of modality to a difference of principle, has the effect of minimizing differences of degree, of more or less equalizing terms which differ from one another only in intensity, and of accentuating that which separates them from the terms of another order. On the other hand, transformation of differences of order into differences of degree has the reverse effect; it brings terms which seemed to be separated by an impassable boundary closer together and emphasizes distances between the degrees.[42]

The defenders of the Marshall Plan, established for a Europe ravaged by war and conceived as a plan of reconstruction, claimed that if the credits were reduced by 25 percent, the plan would turn into a mere program of "welfare": a quantitative difference was presented as a difference of nature. But at what point does a quantitative difference become qualitative? How many hairs must be plucked from a hairy man for him to become bald? At some point a decision must be made by which a difference of degree is transformed into a difference of nature.

In periodizations of history continued and gradual differences are transformed into differences of nature. The Middle Ages differ from the Renaissance and modern times in an essential way, and not simply in nuance. These periods become separated by decisive events which justify their severance. The beginning of a new age is always characterized by events so crucial that what comes after is essentially different from what went before. After Jesus, the Christian believes, the destiny of humanity has been radically altered. Every division into periods is based on characteristic value judgments.

On the contrary, the insertion of the human species (as a result of the theory of evolution) into the animal kingdom transforms into a difference of degree what previously stood as an unbridgeable gap, formed by the presence, in man, of a soul of divine origin.

Montaigne, on the one hand, struggling against the importance given to death, showed our entire life to be a series of jolts marking the passage from youth to old age, of which death is only the last.[43] Bossuet, on the other, reduced the distances between men by showing that all are equal in death.[44]

The Stoics established a fundamental difference between virtuous men and others: "The substance of the wrongdoing may be greater or smaller, but the act itself comprises neither the greater nor the smaller. If a pilot loses a vessel loaded with gold rather than a barge loaded with straw, there will be some difference in the amount of the loss, but none in the incompetence of the pilot."[45] An ethic that is based on conformity to principles or to duty will not make quantitative distinctions between acts, as will an ethic that is based on the importance of the consequences of an action.

9. Argumentation by Example, Illustration, and Model

1. Argumentation by Example

To argue by example is to presuppose the existence of certain regularities of which the examples provide a concretization. What can be disputed when there is recourse to examples is the scope of the rule or degree of generalization which justifies the particular case, but not the principle of generalization itself.

From this point of view, argumentation by example does not consider that which is evoked to be unique, to be tied indissolubly to the context from which the described event arises. On the contrary, it seeks in the specific case the law or the structure which the example reveals. Thus a story which tells how a man through his work and talent climbs the social ladder, even if an explicit lesson is not drawn from it, is nonetheless a lesson in optimism and faith in a society which makes such success possible.

If the presentation of one such story leaves us in doubt regarding its bearing, the setting out of a number of examples of the same sort cannot leave any doubt in the mind of the reader: it is a matter of an argument aiming to move from the specific case toward a generalization. This is the irresistible impression given by two attorneys in a play by Marcel Aymé *(La Tête des autres)*. They are "similarly solicitous about their careers, similarly deceived in marriage, similarly hypocritical, naively corrupt, and self-satisfied."[1] St.-John Perse makes use of this technique by using the plural in speaking of "Coliseums," "Castiles," and "Floridas," so as to give what is unique an archetypal value, leading to the generalization.[2]

Argumentation by example is sometimes used to go not from an example to a rule, but to another particular case. Aristotle writes of the following example: "As the Persian kings Darius and Xerxes did not cross the Aegean until after seizing Egypt, the present Persian king will also cross over into Europe if he seizes Egypt."[3]

In this form of argumentation, it is important that the chosen example be incontestable, since it is the reality of that which is called forth that forms the basis of the conclusion. But what ought to be the scope of the latter? In order not to generalize unduly, it is a good idea to start with sufficiently varied examples, so that one runs less risk of going astray in the generalization. John Stuart Mill's canons concerning "concomitant variations" give us valuable methodological directions.

The argument by example, if joined to the argument *a fortiori*, results in the hierarchical example, of which Aristotle provides this instance:

> Everyone honors the wise. The Parians have honored Archilochus, in spite of his bitter tongue; the Chians Homer, though he was not their countryman; the Mytilenaeans Sappho, though she was a woman; the Lacedaemonians actually made Chilion a member of their senate, though they are the least literary of men.[4]

If the argument by example can always be contested, this is not true of the invalidating case, which, unless it is disqualified, requires the rejection or at least the modification of the rule to which it is opposed. This accounts for the importance accorded it in the methodology of Karl Popper.[5]

Use of the same concept to describe diverse cases makes their comparison to each other easy. It seems to result from the very nature of things. It is thanks to language that it appears completely natural to subsume under the same rule situations that have been described in the same way. It is the desire to differentiate situations described by the same term that needs justification.

2. Illustration

Although argumentation by example is used to establish either a prediction or a rule, the specific case plays a completely different role if the rule is already accepted. It essentially serves to illustrate the rule, that is, to give it a certain presence in consciousness. For this reason, while the reality of the example must be incontestable, the illustration must above all strike the imagination. The way the specific case is identified and described depends entirely upon the role it has in the argument. Does it serve to establish a rule through induction, or to give it presence?

Certain writers such as Edgar Allan Poe and Villiers de l'Isle-Adam make good use of this characteristic of illustration to give their fantastic stories credibility. They often begin their stories by announcing a rule which the events they describe are supposed to illustrate.

The transition from example to illustration occurs almost imperceptibly in cases in which a rule is justified before being illustrated. The first examples need to be generally accepted, since their role is to give the rule credibility; the others, once the rule is accepted, will in turn be supported by it.

Descartes uses this double technique of example and illustration skillfully at the beginning of the second part of the *Discourse on Method*. "There is," he writes, "often less perfection in what has been put together bit by bit, and by different masters, than in the work of a single hand."[6] This idea, at the heart of classicism and the centralizing monarchy, was the one by which Descartes opposed both medieval feudalism and the pluralism of the Renaissance. This idea is first justified by the enumeration of what would have seemed obvious to a person of the seventeenth century:

> Thus we see how a building, the construction of which has been undertaken and completed by a single architect, is usually superior in beauty and regularity to those that many have tried to restore by making use of old walls which had been built for other purposes. So, too, those old places which, beginning as villages, have developed in the course of time into great towns, are generally so ill-proportioned in comparison with those an engineer can design at will in an orderly fashion that, even though the buildings taken severally often display as much art as in other places, or even more, yet the disorder is such with a large house here and a small one there, and the streets all tortuous and uneven, that the whole place seems to be the product of chance rather than the design of men who use their reason.[7]

Descartes goes on to show that the laws formulated by a single legislator, such as Lycurgus of Sparta, like the true religion "for which the ordinances come from God alone," cannot but help be superior to that which is the work of many. In presenting these examples, he thus gives some credibility to his own project, which, once the rule is established, seems to be but a simple application of it. For, without such rhetorical precautions, he would seem to be suggesting something farfetched, namely, to discard through methodological doubt "what we learn from books"—at least from those "swollen with the opinions of a variety of authors"—in order to reconstruct singlehandedly a knowledge based on reason, by following the four rules of his method.

It also happens that the specific case, while it illustrates the rule, is used at the same time to state the rule concretely: "A rolling stone gathers no moss." Sometimes the rule is confirmed by comparison between two applied cases. "Difficulties are what show a man's character. Therefore when you encounter a difficulty, remember that God, like a gymnastics teacher, has pitted you against a young and formidable partner."[8]

Sometimes the illustration is not a historical event but a fictitious case imagined by the author, for example, tales of sailors choosing their captain by lot and thereby ridiculing the Athenian democratic rule for choosing their civil magistrates.[9] Describing utopias fulfills the same purpose.

Rhetorical effects can be drawn from an illustration which is intentionally inadequate, as when the described acts belie either the rule or the epithet which precedes their expression. Antony uses *irony* brilliantly in his discourse on the dead Caesar; he repeats over and over again that "Brutus is an honorable man," but then describes in detail his treasonable acts and ingratitude, which testify to the contrary.[10]

3. Model and Antimodel

The specific case, instead of serving as an example or illustration, can also be presented as a model to be imitated. But not just any action is worth imitating; people imitate only those they admire, who have authority or social prestige because of their competence, their functions, and their place in society.

A legal decision that serves as a precedent is obviously based on the rule of justice which requires equal treatment of essentially similar situations. But the judgment which inspires respect will be that of a tribunal which has authority, such as the Supreme Court, or, in default of that, an appellate court.

The argument by model, like the argument from authority, implies that the authority, by its prestige, is a guarantee for the contemplated action. This is why those who become models must pay attention to what they do and say. The discourse in Isocrates' *To Nicocles* is permeated by this idea:

> Let your own level-headedness stand as an example to the rest, realizing that the manners of the whole state are copied from its rulers. You will have evidence of the value of your royal authority when you see that your subjects enjoy easier circumstances and more civilized habits because of your activity.[11]

The model judges on his own what is better, although he in turn can be inspired by a divine model, as was St. Theresa, who sought in her actions to imitate Jesus. But the discernment of all imitators cannot be counted upon; some may only be able to imitate the weaknesses of their model:

> The example of Alexander's chastity has not made so many continent as that of his drunkenness has made intemperate. It is not shameful not to be as virtuous as he, and it seems excusable to be no more vicious.[12]

Being a model, one can inadvertently provide the model of something else—an idealized image elaborated by the person taking one for a model.

If an inferior person imitating a model has any tendency to resemble him by popularizing the model's behavior, he thereby makes it less distinguished. From this follows the phenomenon of fashion and its periodic revolutions— opposed to the relative stability of dress typical of a specific class. When the maid dresses like a society woman, it is time for the latter to draw the line and change the style.

We thus pass from the model to the antimodel. If the inferior imitates the superior, the latter does not at all wish to resemble the former, who is despised and cited as an example of bad taste and low life. Montaigne was very sensitive to the argument by the antimodel:

> There may be some people of my temperament, I who learn better by contrast than by example, and by flight than by pursuit. This was the sort of teaching that Cato the Elder had in view when he said that the wise have more to learn from the fools than the fools from the wise; and also that ancient lyre player who, Pausanias tells us, was accustomed to force his pupils to go hear a bad musician who lived across the way, where they might learn to hate his discords and false measures. [13]

It is enough to point out the conduct of an antimodel to distinguish oneself from it. The Chevalier de Méré describes the effect of the antimodel on conduct:

> I notice too that we do not merely avoid people we do not like, but hate everything connected with them and wish to resemble them as little as possible. If they praise peace, they make us wish for war; if they are pious and live well-ordered lives, we want to be dissolute and disorderly. [14]

But if the desire to resemble the model provides an adequate directive, there are many ways to avoid the antimodel. The context indicates the direction to be followed: If you don't want to be like Sancho Panza, you may instinctively relate to Don Quixote.

The antimodel is the point of departure for the argument *a contrario* and can be employed for the argument *a fortiori*. If wild beasts are devoted to their young, it would be indecent for men not to exhibit a similar devotion.

The role of model and antimodel is best seen when one is

certain of having found their unquestionable incarnations, as in God and Satan. This is why religiously inspired morality defines the just as an imitation of God and conformity to his commandments.

The advantage of the perfect model is that it requires no discernment: it is enough to be inspired by it to be on the right track. But nothing prevents us from adapting the divine model, if necessary, to the role we want it to play. Bossuet, in many passages, presents Jesus as a model for kings: "to give all monarchs who depend on his power an example of moderation and justice, he desired to make himself subject to the regulations he made, and the laws he established."[15] In another sermon Bossuet says: "This great God knows all things and sees all things and yet he would that all men speak to him; he listens to everything, his ear is always open to the complaints laid before him, and he is ever ready to do justice. There is the model for kings."[16]

Locke believed God to be the model of tolerance; being all powerful, he could compel all men to salvation, but we know that he does not save men against their wills.[17] The Chevalier de Méré held that Jesus, through his actions and discourses, showed us how important it is to please because the love of God extends only to those who please him. On the other hand, Simone Weil underscores the importance the parables give the life of the fields, and draws from this the conclusion that Christianity is a religion which exalts peasants and the products of the earth, bread and wine.[18]

The richness of argumentation by model is that, even when the model is unique, it allows us to accentuate one or another of its aspects and to draw each time a lesson that is adapted to the circumstances.

10. Analogy and Metaphor

THE CONCEPTION AND the role of analogy have varied in the history of philosophy. Whereas for certain thinkers such as Plato or St. Thomas analogy presents a specific and indispensable type of reasoning, for others such as the empiricists, it is limited to affirming a weak resemblance and is useful for formulating hypotheses, but must be eliminated in the formulation of the results of scientific research.

A theoretician of argumentation will maintain that recourse to analogy constitutes one of the characteristics of communication and nonformal reasoning; that in certain cases analogy can, in the long run, be eliminated, when the conclusion arrived at is given in a mathematical formula. Very often, however, especially in philosophy and the expression of religious thought, analogy is at the center of an original vision either of the universe or of the relationship between man and the divine.

However that may be, to preserve its specificity, analogy must be interpreted in terms of its etymological meaning of *proportion*. It differs from the purely mathematical proportion insofar as it does not posit the *equality* of two relations but rather affirms a *similitude* between them. Whereas in algebra positing $a/b = c/d$ makes it possible to affirm $c/d = a/b$ symmetrically and to bring out, on these terms, mathematical operations which result in equations (e.g., $ad - cb = 0$), in analogy we affirm that a is to b as c is to d. It is no longer a question of division but of the comparison of some relationship to another. Between the pairs *a - b* (the *theme* of the analogy) and *c - d* (the *phoros* of the analogy), one does not assert an equality that is by definition symmetrical, but a comparison that has as its purpose the clarification, structuring, and evaluation of the *theme* in terms of what one knows of the *phoros*. This implies that the *phoros* comes from a region that is different from that of the theme and better known than it.

In this perspective, analogy is a part of the theory of argumentation and not of ontology. In certain cases, after an analogy has allowed a scientist to orient his investigations, which in turn have given him experimental results according to which he will structure the theme independently of the phoros, he can abandon the analogy, as does the contractor who takes down the scaffolding after the building is finished. Thus, after the analogy established between electric and hydraulic current gave direction to the first experiments in this field, further experimentation could finally develop in an independent way. In other cases, the analogy will be surpassed, theme and phoros both being reduced to a more general law. But in fields where recourse to empirical methods is impossible, analogy cannot be dispensed with, and the argument that is used will be employed mainly to support it and show its adequacy.

Here are three examples of indispensable analogies borrowed in turn from ethics, metaphysics, and theology. The first is an exhortation by Epictetus.

> If a child puts his hand into a narrow-necked jar to pull out figs and nuts and fills his hand, what will happen to him? He will not be able to pull it out, and he will cry. "Let a few go," someone will tell him, "and you will get your hand out." So I say to you, do the same with your desires. Wish only for a small number of things, and you will obtain them.[1]

Secondly, Leibniz, wishing to clarify the dependence of the other monads on the divine monad, writes in his *Discourse on Metaphysics* "that all other substances depend on God, as thoughts emanate from our substance."[2]

Finally, Joannes Scotus Erigena uses the relation of eyes to light to make us understand the relation between divine grace and human freedom:

> Indeed just as a man when surrounded by thick darkness, though he possesses the sense of sight, sees nothing, because he cannot until there comes from without the light, which he feels even when he keeps his eyes shut, and which he sees, together with all that surrounds him, when he opens his eyes; so is the will of man, as long as he remains in the shadow of original sin and of his own sins, hemmed in by his own darkness. But when the light of divine mercy appears, it not only disperses the night of sin and its guilt, but it heals the sick will, gives it sight, and makes it able to contemplate this light by cleansing it through good works.[3]

These three examples illustrate the role of analogy, which is to clarify the theme through the phoros; in the latter two, to explain an unknown relationship through another more familiar one, and, in the first, to guide men by means of phoros derived from childhood about which adults unanimously agree.

The analogy in four terms can be expressed by means of three terms, one of them being repeated in the theme and in the phoros. Its scheme will be: b is to c as a is to b. Heraclitus noted that "in the sight of the divinity man is as puerile as a child is in the sight of a man."[4] This same structure of three terms is stated in the previously cited passage of Leibniz, as well as in the myth of the cave in book VII of Plato's *Republic*.

For analogy to fulfill its primary role of clarifying the

theme by the phoros, the fields of each must not be homogeneous, as they are in mathematical proportions. In a proportion there is no interaction between the terms; however, this is not the case in analogy. Concerning the annulled election of Amadeus, duke of Savoy, as Pope, Calvin writes that "the aforesaid Amadeus was appeased by a cardinal's hat, as a barking dog by a morsel."[5] Bringing together the disappointed duke and the barking dog devalues, at the same time, the erstwhile pope and the reward that was given to him.

This sort of comparison becomes comical when it happens without the intention and contrary to the will of the author of the analogy. Lawrence Sterne, who in his *Life and Opinions of Tristram Shandy* draws comical effects from the use of maladroit schemes of argumentation, gives us the following exchange:

> —Brave! brave by heaven! cried my uncle *Toby*—he [King William] deserves a crown—As richly, as a thief a halter; shouted *Trim*.[6]

To say that every exploit merits compensation as every crime merits punishment is a serious affirmation, but to say that King William merits a crown as a thief the rope makes us laugh because of the incongruity of the comparison.

When antithetical terms such as "left-right" and "superficial-profound" are regularly used as phores to describe a political position or the expression of a thought one either esteems or belittles, these terms, neutral to begin with, acquire a positive or negative connotation through the role that they regularly play. But when the same term performs various roles in diverse phores, the term will sometimes be evaluated positively and sometimes negatively. In Ezekiel 11:19 (NEB), "I will give them a different heart and put a new spirit into them; I will take the heart of stone out of their bodies and give them a heart of flesh," the "heart of stone" is the symbol of defiance and the "heart of flesh" of pious obedience. But when in Romans 8 St. Paul opposes the flesh to the spirit, the flesh is the symbol of sin and the spirit that of grace. The term "flesh" is thus accorded value in the one analogy and devalued in the other.

It often happens that one or another element of the phoros is modified so as to bring it closer to the theme and render the analogy more convincing. To the degree that the medieval artist wanted to present Moses as a prefiguration of Christ, he shows the prophet astride a donkey with his wife walking behind (contrary to the biblical text) to show a parallel with the entry of Christ into Jerusalem.[7] Similarly, Bossuet, speaking of the compact battalions of Spanish infantry, says that they were as undaunted as towers, but towers "which knew how to repair their breaches."[8]

If someone took these modifications of the phoros literally, he would at times affirm an untruth and at times describe a fantastic reality. But there are limits to such procedures. When the affirmation concerning the phoros seems inadmissible because it is shocking to common sense, we have the type of expressions which Quintilian ridiculed, for example: "Even the sources of mighty rivers are navigable" and "the generous tree bears fruit while it is yet a sapling."[9]

A rich analogy can be extended in a fruitful way. La Bruyère knew how to draw happy effects from such an analogy:

> The wheels, the springs, the movements are hidden: nothing of a watch appears but its hands, which insensibly move round and finish their circuit: the image of a courtier, all the more perfect as, after having covered enough ground, he often returns to the same point from which he set out.[10]

The extension of an analogy will often be useful in

argumentation. Thus the difficulties found at the "base" of knowledge can be compared to a ship tossed about by a storm, and the fact of ending with skeptical conclusions to that of bringing the boat to the bank, where it can remain and rot. Contrasting his methodology with Hume's, Kant says in the *Prolegomena:* "My object is rather to give [this ship] a pilot, who by means of safe astronomical principles drawn from a knowledge of the globe, and provided with a complete chart and a compass, may steer the ship safely whither he listeth."[11] Opposing the normal usage of a boat to the role to which Hume reduced it, Kant underscores, through his analogy, the superiority of his critical philosophy over Hume's skepticism.

Every analogy highlights certain relationships and leaves others in the shadows. With good reason Max Black has emphasized that describing a battle with terms borrowed from checkers disregards all the horrors of war.[12]

In accepting an analogy one subscribes to a certain choice of aspects which it is important to emphasize in the description of a phenomenon. At the same time, in criticizing an author, one is often led to oppose the analogies he uses. Willis Moore, in opposing Wittgenstein's ideas concerning the relations between statements and facts, writes: "If a statement did represent its fact as a line on a record records its sound, we probably should have to agree with Wittgenstein's contention."[13]

In criticizing a thesis illustrated by an analogy, we must either adapt the analogy so that it corresponds better to our own conceptions, or replace it by another, thought to be more adequate. The two procedures are found in controversies.

Thus Leibniz, in his discussion with Locke, does not accept the conception which holds that the mind, in knowledge, plays a role analogous to a clear piece of marble upon which experience leaves its traces; rather, its role is analogous to a veined piece of marble that is therefore predisposed to receive one figure rather than another.[14]

On the other hand, when the criticized analogy is in its essentials opposed to the way in which we understand the theme, we will be led, in order to express our own point of view, to replace the disputed phoros by another, more adequate one. Since M. Polanyi conceives of scientific activity as systematic, he opposes Milton's analogy in the *Areopagitica,* which likens the activities of learned men to those who attempt to recover the fragments of a broken statue; for Polanyi, scientific activity is analogous to the development of a living organism.[15]

Aristotle defines metaphor as "giving the thing a name belonging to something else, the transference being either from genus to species or from species to genus, or from species to species, or on grounds of analogy."[16] Although Aristotle considers every trope a metaphor, we will limit ourselves to the last case he envisages: for us, a metaphor is only a condensed analogy, due to a fusion of theme and phoros. From the analogy *a* is to *b* as *c* is to *d,* the metaphor takes one of these forms: *a* of *d, c* of *b, a* is *c.* From the classical example of analogy, "old age is to life what the evening is to the day," we derive the metaphors "old age of the day," "evening of life," or "old age is an evening."

The metaphors of the form *a* is *c* are the most deceiving because we are tempted to see an identification in them, although we can understand them satisfactorily only by reconstructing the analogy and supplying the missing terms. Let us note that this kind of metaphor can be expressed in an even more condensed way and can result from the confrontation between a modifying term and the reality to which it applies. In writing "this lion charged" about a courageous warrior, we understand that "this warrior" is a "lion," which is made explicit by the analogy "this warrior in relation to other men is as a lion in relation to other animals." In a more general way, "when we say of a man that he is a bear, a lion, a wolf, a pig, or a lamb, we metaphorically describe his character, his behavior, or his place among other people in keeping with the idea we have of the behavior or place of such a species in the animal world, attempting to arouse in relation to him the same reactions which we ordinarily experience in relation to these species."[17]

The metaphorical fusion, which tends to assimilate the domain of the theme to that of the phoros, especially in order to create a poetic emotion, allows better than analogy for the back and forth movement wherein the theme and the phoros become, so to speak, indivisible. In the celebrated "Ode à Cassandre," Ronsard, before describing the young girl as if she were a rose, begins by presenting the rose in terms that fit a young girl:

> Mignonne, allons voir si la rose
> Qui ce matin avait déclose
> Sa robe de pourpre au soleil,
> A point perdue ceste Vesprée,
> Les plis de sa robe pourpée
> Et son teint au vostre pareil.

> [Sweetheart, come see if the rose,
> Which this morning began to unclose
> Its damask gown to the sun,
> Has not lost, now day is done,
> The folds of its damasked gown,
> And its colors so like your own.][18]

This metaphorical fusion can be indicated by an adjective (a *luminous* exposé), a verb (he *shot back* a reply), a possessive (*our* Waterloo), a determination (the evening *of life*), the copula (life *is* a dream), or even by the employment of a single word in a context which excludes its literal meaning.[19]

Metaphors become worn out by repetition, and we have a tendency to forget that we are dealing with metaphors: we say of them, metaphorically, that they are "dead" or "dormant." Having become an ordinary manner of expression, their metaphorical aspect reappears when we want to translate them into a foreign language which does not contain the same forms. When the metaphorical expression is the sole way to designate an object in a language, it is called a *catachresis:* the "*foot* of a mountain" and "*arm* of a chair."

Recourse to catachresis is very effective in argumentation because, by drawing a conclusion from a habitual manner of expression, the reader does not perceive the expression's analogous character; the conclusion seems to flow from the nature of things. Thus Descartes in the Seventh Rule for the direction of the mind exploits the catachresis "the chain of ideas," stressing that in a rigorous deduction it is necessary never to skip any link of the chain, for "when the least part that you choose is omitted, the whole chain is immediately broken, and all the certainty of the conclusion falls to the ground."[20] But if we alter the phoros, so that reasoning is not likened to a "chain" but to a "cloth" of which the web is made of interlaced arguments, we immediately see that its strength is far superior to each of its threads, and we can no longer affirm that it is analogous to a chain, which is no stronger than its weakest link.[21]

There are many ways to use the same metaphor, each highlighting different aspects and leading to different conclusions. Method is often described as a road (this recalls the etymology of the word "method"), but each thinker uses this description in his own way. In the second part of the *Discourse on Method,* Descartes writes: "Like a man who walks alone in the darkness, I resolved to go so slowly and circumspectly that if I did not get ahead very rapidly I was at least safe from falling."[22]

Leibniz, on the other hand, emphasizes the social aspect of knowledge. Writing that "the human race, considered in relation to the sciences which contribute to our happiness, resembles a troupe of people who march in confusion in the darkness, without leader, order, cadence, or any other means for keeping in step or for recognizing each other," he advises us to "stay in line and march in step, share the highways, point out the roads and maintain them."[23]

For these two classical thinkers, science is complete in God's mind: the road is completely laid out, it is enough simply to follow it. For Hegel, on the contrary, the road continues to be constructed as knowledge progresses. Personally, wishing to give greater importance to tradition, initiative, and practice in the growth of knowledge, I have written that "our intellectual advance is aided by our parents and teachers; before building new roads or improving old ones, we have used a great number of roads, laid out by the generations which preceded us; that because of neglect certain roads decay and are covered with vegetation which makes us lose track of them; that we are often happy to rediscover them after many centuries of disuse; that certain roads are so steep that only mountain climbers who are well equipped and highly trained can venture upon them."[24]

We see by these examples that the description of the theme does not depend only upon the choice of the phoros, but also that the idea we have of the theme can guide the manner by which the same phoros will develop.

The danger of certain metaphors, such as a "*bouquet* of wings" to designate a bird, a "*vessel* of scales" to designate a fish, is to take them for images which would evoke some fantastic being, such as a "*thinking* reed." It is this error which I.A. Richards, some time ago, justly denounced.[25]

By virtue of being continuously used as phores in the same metaphors, certain terms have their metaphorical meaning become their ordinary meaning. The terms "clear" or "murky" immediately seem to describe a thought or quality and a liquid. But what seems a cliché or ordinary usage recovers its metaphorical meaning by means of varied stylistic techniques. A. Henry has analyzed these with great finesse.[26]

Juxtaposing two clichés will produce a surprising effect, even laughter: That top banana is the cream of society. Often an allusion or an opposition suffices. The most interesting technique for argumentation, however, consists in developing a dormant metaphor, drawing it out in order to give to the style an uncommonly suggestive force. This technique was often used by La Bruyère and also by Pascal, as we can see by this thought: "The great and the humble have the same misfortunes, the same griefs, the same passions; but the one is at the top of the wheel, and the other near the center, and so less disturbed by the same revolution."[27]

The expression "to be at a dead end" again becomes metaphoric in this statement by Bachelard: "Instead of being a dead end, as the earlier psychology proclaimed, abstraction is an intersection of avenues."[28]

Today, whether it is a question of metaphors living or dead, awakened or dormant, the certainty prevails that philosophic thought, and perhaps all creative thought, cannot do without them. This idea, which perhaps had its beginnings in the work of Nietzsche, has been widespread for more than thirty years in Anglo-American thought. For S.C. Pepper, the varied visions of the world are distinguished by "root metaphors."[29] These are the metaphors which, according to Dorothy Emmet, characterize metaphysical thought.[30] Philip Wheelwright takes up this same idea in two well-known works, *The Burning Fountain* (1954) and *Metaphor and Reality* (1962). Douglas Berggren, following the same tendency further in an important article, "The Use and Abuse of Metaphor," concludes that article by writing that "truly creative and non-mythic thought, whether in the arts, the sciences, religion, or metaphysics, must be invariably and irreducibly metaphorical."[31]

Finally, in Germany H. Blumenberg is working out a "metaphorology," a new discipline which he sees as occupying a central place in the study of cultures and systems of thought.[32]

Is all philosophy, as Derrida (following Nietzsche) would have it, only the deceptive utilization of an absolute and abstract truth, set all the while in the prolongation of a myth?[33] Or is it, as Ricoeur claims, the choice and development of a *living* metaphor?[34] It doesn't matter. What is certain is that philosophical thought, incapable of empirical verification, develops by an argumentation that aims to have certain analogies and metaphors accepted as central elements in a world view.

11. The Dissociation of Ideas

IN THE SIXTH CHAPTER, where we first spoke of the dissociation of ideas, we pointed out that this argumentative technique is hardly mentioned in traditional rhetoric, since it is a method that is indispensable chiefly to those who analyze philosophical thought, that is, thought which tries to be systematic. When, faced with the incompatibilities that ordinary thought encounters, a person does not limit himself to conjuring away the difficulty by pretending not to see it, but instead tries to resolve it in a theoretically satisfying manner by reestablishing a coherent vision of reality, he will most often attain such a resolution by a dissociation of the ideas accepted at the start. Thus Kant, seeing that the method of the natural sciences assumes universal determinism and that of the moral sciences the freedom of the responsible agent, and trying to resolve the antinomy that results from this double perspective, dissociates the idea of reality into phenomenal reality, ruled by universal determinism, and noumenal reality, where causality rules through freedom.[1] This dissociation into phenomenal reality (reality as it appears) and into noumenal reality (of things in themselves) is a typical instance of using the pair appearance/reality, a practice which we find directly or indirectly in all dissociations.

At first sight, appearance is nothing but a manifestation of reality: it is reality as it appears, as it presents itself to immediate experience. But when appearances are incompatible—when, for example, the oar is plunged into the water and appears broken to our sight and straight when we touch it—they cannot represent reality as it is, since reality is governed by the principle of noncontradiction and cannot simultaneously, and in the same relationship, have and not have a given property. It is therefore essential to distinguish between appearances which correspond to reality and those which do not and are deceptive. Hence appearance will have an equivocal status: sometimes it is the expression of reality, at other times only the source of error and illusion. Whereas appearance is given, immediate, the beginning of knowledge, reality, which, when it is known, is normally known only through appearances, becomes the criterion that allows us to judge them. Reality will be "term II," which will be normative in relation to "term I," to the very extent that it confirms term I as the authentic expression of the real or disqualifies it as error and false appearance. With the model of the appearance/reality pair we can present the philosophical pairs in the form of the pair term I/term II.

Term I corresponds to the apparent, to what occurs in the first instance, to what is actual, immediate, and known directly. Term II, to the extent that it is distinguished from it, can be understood only by comparison with term I: it results from a dissociation effected within term I with the purpose of getting rid of the incompatibilities that may appear between different aspects of term I. Term II provides a criterion, a norm which allows us to distinguish those aspects of term I which are of value from those which are not; it is not simply a datum, it is a *construction* which, during the dissociation of term I, establishes a rule that makes it possible to classify the multiple aspects of term I in a hierarchy. It enables those that do not correspond to the rule which *reality* provides to be termed illusory, erroneous, or apparent (in the depreciatory sense of this word). In relation to term I, term II is both normative and explanatory. After the dissociation has been made, term II makes it possible to retain or to disqualify the various aspects under which term I is presented. It makes it possible to distinguish, out of a number of appearances of doubtful status, whose which are mere appearances and those which represent reality.

This point seems to us essential because of its importance in argumentation. While the original status of what is presented as the starting point of the dissociation is unclear and undetermined, the dissociation into terms I and II will attach value to the aspects that correspond to term II and will lower the value of the aspects that are in opposition to it. Term I, appearance in the strict sense of the word, is mere illusion and error.

In actual fact, term II is not always accompanied by a precise criterion that makes separation of the various aspects of term I possible. The standard it provides can only be potential, and its principal effect is to order the terms resulting from the dissociation in a hierarchy. Kant, in order to resolve the cosmological antinomies, dissociated reality and distinguished between phenomena and things in themselves. The term II he constructed in this way is not known, but this did not prevent the phenomenal world, conditioned by our power of knowledge, from being devalued as compared to the reality of things in themselves. Term II profits from its oneness, from its coherence, when set against the multiplicity and incompatibility of the aspects of term I, some of which will be disqualified and marked ultimately for disappearance.

In term II, then, reality and value are closely linked. This connection is specifically pronounced in all the constructions of metaphysicians.[2]

The opposition between reality and appearance is equally manifest in everyday thought in the opposition between the object and its shadow, between the world of wakefulness and the world of dream, and between lived reality and what is only theatrical representation.

It is by analogy with the appearance/reality pair of common sense that metaphysicians such as Plato and Plotinus devalue the sensible world in order to contrast it to true reality, to the world of ideas or of the transcendent.

In the myth of the cave in the seventh book of the *Republic,* Plato shows us that sensible realities are in the same relation to the world of ideas that shadows cast by objects are in relation to the objects themselves. It is the world of ideas which constitutes true reality, term II in relation to the appearances (term I) which our senses furnish us.

Plotinus compares life and death to sleep and wakefulness: "but the true wakening is a true getting up from the body, not with the body. Getting up with the body is only getting out of one sleep into another, like getting out of one bed into another; but the true rising is a rising altogether from the body" (*Enneads* 3.6.6, trans. Armstrong).

Plotinus deprecates earthly life by comparing it to a game, to a spectacle.

"For reality here in the events of our life it is not the soul within but the outside shadow of man which cries and carries on in every sort of way on a stage which is the whole earth where men have in many places set up their stages. Doings like these belong to a man who knows how to live only the lower and external life and is not aware that he is playing in his tears, even when they are serious tears. For only the seriously good part of man is capable of taking serious thoughts seriously; the rest of man is a toy. (*Enneads* 3.2.15, trans. Armstrong)

On the basis of the opposition of term I/term II as it appears, for example, in the *Phaedrus,* Plato's philosophical system develops through a series of value judgments,

starting from the pair material world/world of ideas, and
moving through the derived pairs, opinion/knowledge;
sensible knowledge/rational knowledge; body/soul; becom-
ing/immutability; plurality/oneness; human/divine.[3] All
philosophical thought can be presented in the form of a
string of pairs which form a system: we have elsewhere
shown this for Spinoza and Marx.[4] The influence on
Western thought of the great metaphysical systems is
marked by the fact that, faced with each philosophical pair,
we hardly hesitate to attribute to each member of the pair
the place of term I or II. Thus common sense freely presents
the traditional pairs: means/end; consequence/fact (or
principle); act/person; accident/essence; occasion/cause;
relative/absolute; subjective/objective; multiplicity/unity;
average/norm; individual/universal; particular/general;
theory/practice; language/thought; letter/spirit.[5]

But an original thought can quickly bring about a reversal
of the terms of a pair. Rarely, however, does this reversal
take place without a modification of one or the other term,
for it is a matter of pointing out the reasons which justify this
reversal. Thus the pair individual/universal, which is characteristic of traditional metaphysics, if reversed, gives the
pair abstract/concrete. In fact, the individual, who alone is
concrete, is accorded value when the universal is considered
not as a superior reality, a Platonic idea, but as an
abstraction derived from the concrete. But in this case it is
the immediately given which becomes the real, the abstract
being only a derivative and theoretical elaboration corresponding to the pair theory/reality.

Another example of pair reversal is found in the work of
Henri Bergson, who reversed the pair act/essence into
essence (or form)/becoming. Here is how Bergson accomplished it:

> Now, life is an evolution. We concentrate a period of this
> evolution in a stable view which we call a form.... There

is no form, since form is immobile, and the reality is movement. What is real is the *continual change* of form: *form is only a* snapshot view of a transition.... When the successive images do not differ from each other too much, we consider them all as the waxing and waning of a single mean image or as the deformation of the image in different directions. And to this mean we really allude when we speak of the essence of a thing, or of the thing itself.[6]

Only the changing is real, concrete; the form would be only an abstraction, a creation of the mind.

This tendency to grant primacy to the concrete, to the immediately given, ends necessarily in a devaluation of the real, defined as a mental construct, into illusion, mere myth. One finds this in thinkers who are suspicious of metaphysics, which leads to multiple and opposing visions of reality. It is in Schopenhauer, and even more so in Nietzsche. It characterizes contemporary positivist and existentialist currents of thought. A passage from Sartre brings this out clearly:

Modern thought has realized considerable progress by reducing the existent to the series of appearances which manifest it.... The appearances which manifest the existent are neither interior nor exterior; they are all equal, they all refer to other appearances, and none of them is privileged.... The dualism of being and appearance is no longer entitled to any legal status within philosophy. The appearance refers to the total series of appearances and not to a hidden reality which would drain to itself all the *being* of the existent.

To the extent that men had believed in noumenal realities, they have presented appearances as a pure negative.... But if we once get away from what Neitzsche called "the illusion of a world-behind-the-scene" and if we no longer believe in the being-behind-the-appearance, then the appearance becomes full positivity; its essence is an "appearing" which is no longer opposed to being but is on the contrary the measure of it. For the being of an existent is exactly what *appears*. . . . The essence of an existent . . . is the manifest law which presides over the succession of its appearances; it is the principle of the series. . . . But essence, as the principle of the series, is definitely only the concatenation of appearances that is, itself, an appearance. . . . Thus the phenomenal being manifests itself; it manifests its essence as well as its existence, and it is nothing but the well-connected series of its manifestations.[7]

Sartre, in order to reject the dissociation between appearance and reality, the dualism of being and appearance, uses a technique of reasoning analogous to that Bergson used in order to find in essence only a "mean" image which strongly resembles "the principle of the series." But because he refuses to see true reality in Bergsonian "becoming," he does not accord *essence* the status of term I in a pair.

All the same, Sartre cannot defend the thesis that appearances are never deceiving, so what is it that distinguishes appearances which are deceiving from those which are not? Sartre gets around this problem by employing a philosophical pair from Hegelian and Marxist dialectic, corresponding to the pair abstract/concrete, according to which it is the infinite series of appearances that allows one to assess them individually. This gives us a pair part/whole, the part being only an abstraction in relation to the total series of appearances. The primacy accorded to the concrete conceived as a totality, all the while pretending to reject all duality, every philosophical pair, simply reintroduces it in a new way through the distinction between the totality of the series and each of its elements. This recalls Bergson's conception, according to which the true length of an object would not be the length which is hidden behind the operations of measurement, but an average magnitude, resulting from a series of measures, and which would be the most probable magnitude statistically. While claiming to reject all duality between being and appearing, this only puts aside one type of dualism, all the while introducing it in another form, closer to scientific procedures.

The pair means/end can be easily made to correspond to the pair appearance/reality. In fact, when it concerns choosing a course of conduct, it is easy to disqualify a desired goal by showing that the goal is only apparent, actually only a means of realizing a more distant end. It is the end which becomes the criterion through which one can judge the adequate character of an act: its transformation into a means relativizes it in relation to the sought-for end. This end, however, could be disqualified, in turn, as but a means toward a still more distant end. If we do not find the final end, which will put a stop to this dialectic of ends and means, we will be entirely enmeshed in circumstances which in the long run take away all sense from existence. From this we understand Buber's disdain of the means/end pair, which is derived from "the useful," from our attitude toward things which are a part of the domain of the *It:*

> The development of the ability to experience and use comes about mostly through the decrease of man's power to enter into relation. . . . The unbelieving core in the self-willed man can perceive nothing but unbelief and self-will, establishing of a purpose and devising of a means. Without sacrifice and without grace, without meeting and without presentness, he has as his world a mediated world, cluttered with purposes.[8]

This whole development only serves to contrast the *personal* relationship—the encounter with "the other," human love and the love of God—to instrumental relationships with things. Rejecting the two terms of the means/end pair leads to setting up the It/Thou pair, and to according value to interpersonal relationships, modeled on the personal relationship *par excellence* that one establishes with God. In this example, the rejection of the means/end duality leads equally to another philosophical pair: relation with things/relations with persons, where term I is discredited because it is the sign of a life without love and dignity.

Reasoning by dissociation is characterized from the start by the opposition of appearance and reality. This dissociation can be applied to any idea, as soon as one makes use of the adjectives "apparent" or "illusory" on the one hand, and "real" or "true" on the other. To use an expression such as "apparent peace" or "true democracy" is to point out the absence of "true" peace, the presence of "apparent" democracies: one adjective is a reflex of the other.

Other adjectives referring to pairs derived from the appearance/reality pair are: opinion/truth; name/thing; artifice/nature; convention/reality; subject/object; letter/spirit. All equally indicate the presence of a dissociation.

Prefixes such as *pseudo* (pseudo-atheist),[9] *quasi* (quasi-multiplicity),[10] *non* (nonphilosophy);[11] the adjective *pretended*, and the use of quotation marks indicate that term I is at issue, whereas capital letters (Being), the definite article (*the* solution), and the adjectives *unique* or *true* point to term II.[11]

Let us cite a passage from a study on Mauriac. Without referring explicitly to philosophical pairs, it spontaneously develops around an opposition between terms I and II of a pair which we have only to reconstruct. We italicize the words which refer to it:

> There is in Mauriac something audacious and *authentic*—we might aptly say unpolluted—a personal *integrity*, a *kernel of purity*, which does not allow him to be intimidated or *led astray* by the world and social life.... But all that which is purely social *superstructure*, leaves him, to put it mildly, indifferent: we have seen with what

virulence he cudgels "proprieties," compromises, and prejudices.... He detests castes ... factitious groupings... The world *pollutes pure* nature formed by the Creator.... His *real* frame [of reference] is free nature.... Need one remind the reader of all those people who in drawing room or bar—in the *spurious* and *artificial* atmosphere of the "world"—suddenly feel themselves overwhelmed by an immense wave of despair?... Mauriac is always for the *truth* against the lie, for the *spirit* against *tradition,* for the *genuineness* of direct person-to-person relations.... And it is this *inborn* nobility, this honest purity, this incorruptible *ingenuousness,* this fearless resolve to denounce every *falsification* which makes any work by Mauriac sound like a pressing appeal to what is most *sincere* and throbbingly alive deep within us.... It is all this too—this undisguised *genuineness,* this bold, open absence of *mask* and *armor* which brings Mauriac, with all great sense of equity and candor, into contact with unbelievers, despite his absolute Catholicism.[13]

In this text, in which philosophical pairs are nowhere mentioned, we cannot fail to reconstruct the romantic pair social/personal by which term II indicates what is innate and natural, sincere and authentic, while every social participation is only superficial and artificial, a "mask" and an "armor" behind which we have to rediscover the true person.

A writer does not have to make explicit reference to a philosophical pair or one of its terms for the reader to introduce a dissociation spontaneously, when faced with a text that would be incoherent and tautological, and hence insignificant, without it. In fact, the reader, showing a certain good will toward the author, presumes that the author is not amusing himself by knowingly asserting incoherent ideas or propositions that are not worth communicating. This can be illustrated by this couplet by

Schiller:

> What religion do I profess? None of these
> That you mention.—And why none?—For Religion's
> sake![14]

True religion prevents adherence to any actual religion.
Another example is given by Cocteau:

> The ink I use is the blue blood of a swan,
> Who dies when he must in order to be more alive.[15]

The figure called *paradoxism,* wherein an antithesis is formulated "by uniting words that appear to be mutually exclusive,"[16] is also understandable only through an effort at dissociation.

It is the same with expressions that are called *apparent* tautologies and that derive their meaning only from the reinterpretation of one of the terms through a dissociation. Thus sayings like "boys will be boys" or "business is business" explain something's happening by reference to what normally happens, the particular case being considered as the expression of an essence.[17]

When respect for the author is such that it is impossible that he could be mistaken, being faced with what seems an error requires the reader to seek a true meaning, which will no longer be the literal one. Pascal wrote, "When the word of God, which is really true, is false literally, it is true spiritually."[18] The solution to the incompatibility is furnished by the pair letter/spirit.

All the definitions which Charles Leslie Stevenson, in a thought-provoking article, called "persuasive"—and which contrast a novel, "true" meaning to a customary but specious one—set up a dissociation of the defined idea.[19] Recourse to such definitions is common in the writings of philosophers, who are led to redefine ideas from common language in order to adapt them to their own systems.[20] Spinoza explicitly points this out with regard to his own definitions, which do not conform to usage but to the nature of things.[21] It is the same with Berkeley, who, to introduce his paradoxical conception of matter, writes:

> There is no matter, if by that term be meant an unthinking substance existing without the mind: but if by matter is meant some sensible thing, whose existence consists in being perceived, then there is matter.[22]

It is curious to note that the existentialists who, as we have seen in the example of Sartre, are opposed to all types of dualism, do not hesitate to resort to etymology to extol an authentic meaning, which should be the primitive meaning, in preference to the customary one.

We end this chapter by noting that rhetoric, thought of as *behavior* and *artifice,* and as opposed to the romantic's battlehorses *sincerity* and *naturalness,* has been the object of attacks which Jean Paulhan has called "terrorist."[23] Can we not reply to these critics by showing that while their criticism is valid in regard to a static, formalistic, and Scholastic rhetoric, it has no bearing on a persuasive rhetoric, a dynamic adaptation to audiences of all sorts?

12. Fullness of Argumentation
and Strength of Arguments

THE PROBLEM OF fullness is characteristic of argumentation; it does not figure in demonstrative proof. In fact, if the latter has been correctly carried out, it is valid for everybody. The more concise it is, the more elegant it seems, because the same result has been obtained at less expense; however, the value of the demonstration is entirely independent of its length. This is not true of argumentative discourse.

Since argument does not unfold within the framework of a closed system, it is necessary, to begin with, to ascertain whether or not the premises are accepted by the audience. The speaker must reinforce, if possible, the presence of the premises in the hearers' minds, make their meaning and import precise, and draw arguments from them in favor of the thesis he wishes to defend. Since no one argument is compelling, but since each seems to contribute to the reinforcement of the argumentation as a whole, one could believe that the efficacy of the discourse is a function of the number of arguments.

Several reasons, however, are opposed to this optimistic vision of things. Although it is true that the elements interact and at times appreciably reinforce the value of isolated arguments, this impression is not always produced. An argument, if it is not adapted to the audience, can arouse a negative reaction. If it arouses objections that prevail upon the mind of the audience, the argument will seem weak, and this weakness can reflect upon the whole discourse, because the image of the speaker—what Aristotle defined as the oratorical *ethos*—will be changed. The speaker might appear as if he is in bad faith, unworthy of confidence, because of his failure to advance better arguments in favor of the thesis he defends.

Besides, to give reasons in favor of a thesis is to imply that the thesis is not self-evident and does not compel everyone. If it is necessary to prove the existence of God, it is because the matter is contested. If it is necessary to furnish proof of the honesty or the impartiality of a person, it is because these are in question. When a speaker cites an event, he intimates that the event happened, but if (except in an historical work) a speaker quotes the source from which the information is derived, he often seems to suggest that he does not necessarily stand behind the information himself.

Whatever be the benefit of an accumulation of arguments, there are psychological, social, and economic limits that prevent a thoughtless amplification of the discourse. If the discourse is presented in manuscript form, the cost of printing can cause the editor to balk, and a too lengthy book risks discouraging its readers. If it is an oral discourse, the patience and attention of the listeners have limits which it is dangerous to go beyond. If we participate in a debate, we must not forget that the time one speaker uses is taken from the time available to the others. This is the reason why each human group, each institution, has its rules and limits to be respected, which sometimes strictly regulate the time available for speaking.

Since the number of arguments is a priori indefinite, a choice must inevitably be made, guided by the idea one has of the respective arguments. This strength can be evaluated in a very intuitive way, but the idea that we have of it when we try to make it precise seems all the more confused because two qualities are mixed together in it in such a way that they are hard to keep apart. These two qualities are *efficacy* and *validity*. Is the strong argument the one that persuades effectively, or is it the one that must convince every reasonable mind? Since the efficacy of an argument is relative to the audience, it is impossible to evaluate it above and beyond reference to the audience to which it is presented. On the other hand, validity is relative to a competent audience, most often to the universal audience.

The strength of an argument depends upon the adherence of the listeners to the premises of the argumentation; upon the pertinence of the premises; upon the close or distant relationship which they may have with the defended thesis; upon the objections which can be opposed to it; and upon the manner in which they can be refuted.

The strength of arguments, if it cannot be calculated in terms of probability, can be understood to be a function of the audience, of its convictions, of its traditions, and of the methods of reasoning appropriate to it. In evaluating them, it is customary to call upon the rule of formal justice which considers as just and reasonable the treatment of essentially similar situations in the same manner. If an argument has prevailed in a given milieu, the argument *a simili* or *a fortiori* allows us to apply it successfully in a new situation. Methodology informs us of the means of proof acceptable in the context of each discipline. The history of a science informs us not only of the theses and the accepted theories, of the instruments used to determine facts, but also of the techniques of recognized reasoning, the type of arguments accepted as pertinent. Similarly, each philosophy favors certain kinds of arguments and discounts others. We have seen that Utilitarianism considers as solely valid the argument from consequences, while Neoplatonic philosophers prefer to use analogical arguments that are tied to an ontology which puts the diverse aspects of reality in a hierarchy.[1]

Speakers often exhibit a natural tendency toward overvaluing their own arguments and undervaluing the arguments of their opponents. Call it wishful thinking. Thus it is an effective technique to limit the bearing of an argument by settling for a conclusion short of what would appear called for. It inspires confidence.

One lessens or augments the strength of certain arguments or opinions by placing them in the context the person of the speaker gives them. Praise of the opponent, of his talent as a speaker, of his prestige and his skill tends to diminish proportionately the strength of his arguments. It suggests that his discourse, though apparently effective, does not present a valid argumentation for a more critical and less impressionable audience. The same praise or blame will be weakened or reinforced by reference to the habitual severity or indulgence of the person who bestows it.

The known, foreseen, and banal argument, which is nothing more than a commonplace, is less compelling than one that is original, new, and to the point. The audience assumes that the banal argument cannot have been unknown to the opponent who, nevertheless, has adopted the opposite theses. Calling an argument a sophism devalues it. On the other hand, taking up an opponent's argument in order to turn it against him can make it prevail, since using it acknowledges its strength. The spirit of repartee benefits from this element, as it does from the element of surprise. This is the advantage of an argument of Bossuet. To those who, arguing that they have many children to care for, refuse to be generous to the poor, Bossuet retorts:

> This imposes on you the obligation to exercise a more abundant charity, for you have more persons for whose sake you ought to placate God.... If then you love your

children, if you would open to their necessities the source
of a truly fatherly gentleness and love, commend them to
God by your good works.[2]

The speaker who extends the analogy of the opponent and
uses it to his own advantage has a stronger argument at his
disposal than the person who sets one analogy against
another.

The person who begs for a certain type of proof gives
weight to it, because he explicitly admits that his agreement
will depend upon the realization of one or another condition. During a strike, a shrewd American industrialist had
written on a blackboard before the discussions the reasons
for the dissatisfaction of the strikers; this action prevented
the introduction of new elements into the negotiations.[3]

It would be considered bad faith, because of the rule of
justice, if a person acknowledged the value of an argument
when it was to his advantage and denied it when this
argument was turned against him.

If distinct arguments end in the same conclusion, be the
latter general or particular, definitive or provisional, the
value accorded to each isolated argument will undoubtedly
be enhanced. When it is uncontested, the *convergence* of
arguments produces a great persuasive effect. This is
undeniably the case when this convergence occurs in
experimental results; when the same result is obtained by
means of different methods, this *consilience* constitutes the
most solid foundation of inductive reasoning. This is the
way that, by several different methods, Avogadro's number
was agreed upon.[4]

If many idependent testimonies agree on the essential, the
value of each testimony is greatly enhanced, though too
great agreement can evoke suspicion of their independence.
If an improbable event occurs, it can be the result of chance;
but if such events occur often, we seek an explanation which
can more easily make comprehensible such a succession of

improbable events. If the first card of a pack is the ace of hearts and the second the king, we are hardly surprised, but if the third is the queen and the fourth is the jack, we say that the deck has not been shuffled or that the cards have been stacked. Too pat a coincidence leads to suspicion; plebiscites in which the total of "yes" votes is almost 100 percent do not inspire confidence.

It is for this reason that certain divergences are signs of sincerity and seriousness, a proof that the results have not been arranged in advance. The weakness shown by Jesus at the time of his crucifixion is an argument in favor of the authenticity of the Gospel accounts.

The fact that people are always looking for what is favorable to the thesis they defend causes them to label "defeatist" the person who insists on dwelling on things that are unfavorable to the common cause; they wonder whether he does not desire the opponent's victory.

Fullness of argumentation is, of course, often explained by the speaker's ignorance of the theses accepted by the audience. Not knowing which will be effective, one may present several arguments, sometimes complementary and sometimes even incompatible. This may happen in the double defense, in fact and in law, that operates on two levels. In the first instance, a person denies that he committed the acts of which he stands accused; in the second, he tries to show that these acts would be contrary to neither law nor morality. This double defense would be superflous if one or the other argument had been irrefutable. But it can be that doubt about the facts makes legal argumentation more easily acceptable.

In other circumstances a second argument comes to the support of the first. Thus, after having shown that one's opponent is in error—that he has confused reality with appearance—one tries to explain the origin of the error or illusion by invoking passions and interests, imagination or prejudice, which intervened in the formation of his judgment. In effect, it is necessary to show in a plausible way that a convincing argument, which should have been accepted by every reasonable intellect, has made no impression on the opponent. It is thus common for an argument bearing on a case to be complemented by another disqualifying a recalcitrant opponent.

Fullness may result not only from the presentation of varied arguments but from repetition, from the amplification of a single argument. This emphasis has the effect of giving presence to certain arguments. It is sometimes useful, but it risks being tedious.

The fullness of argumentation is not without dangers when it leads to the use of weak, irrelevant, improper, or incompatible arguments. A person introducing a weak argument should mention that it is introduced only as a subsidiary. On the other hand, if the argument seems weak but is not, one can stake his case on it. An accusation of irrelevance can be refuted by showing the unsuspected pertinence of what one puts forth.

In instances of improper arguments, such as self-praise, the speaker should emphasize that the opponent's attitude forced him to use them.[5] Sometimes one can content himself with making allusions to these arguments without developing them. Many rhretorical figures, such as *preterition* or *reticence,* refer to this technique wherein one is content to allude to an argument but to leave its development to the audience's imagination.

On occasion, it is advantageous to give up an argument: this concession to an opponent is proof of good will, of the superabundance of arguments at one's disposal, but which are not used, since the cause that is being defended seems solid. Another concession is to follow the opponent on his ground, taking up, point by point, all the elements of his discourse. It also happens that the speaker can grant the opponent's point, only to go him one better by adding even more arguments to his thesis. This can get comic:

> Domitia complained that, by way of accusing her of meanness, Junius Bassius had alleged that she even sold her old shoes. No, he replied, I never said anything of the sort. I said you bought old shoes.[6]

He who fears to utilize incompatible arguments can in fact decide not to use some of them. But he can also attribute these to different people: Kierkegaard had works which defended opposing theses appear under different pseudonyms.

The problem of fullness and the dangers it poses must be examined in relation to each argumentative situation. They will seem different, depending on whether a speaker is to defend a thesis alone or is to share this task with others, and depending on whether he is content with refuting an opponent's thesis or is seeking to win him to his own cause.

13. The Order of Arguments in a Discourse

UNDER THE NAMES *dispositio* in antiquity and *method* in the Renaissance, rhetoric and dialectic have dealt with the organization of subject matters and the order of arguments in a speech. Different parts were distinguished—the *exordium*, the *narration*, the *proof*, the *refutation*, the *recapitulation*, and the *peroration*—as if all speeches had the same structure, whatever their purpose, audiences, and time available. Aristotle had remarked that the traditional divisions worked only for this or that kind of speech. To him, there were only two indispensable parts: the statement of the thesis that one proposes to defend and the means of proving it.[1] But on this interpretation the order will be essentially limited to that in which the arguments are laid out.

Let us note immediately that order has no importance in a purely formal demonstration; such demonstration is a matter, by means of a correct inference, of transferring to theorems the truth value attributed by hypothesis to axioms. However, order is important in argumentation aimed at obtaining the adherence of an audience. In fact, the order of the presentation of arguments modifies the conditions of their acceptance.

The exordium, although in principle its subject may be irrelevant to the thesis under discussion, is the part of the speech that is treated by almost all the masters of rhetoric. For Aristotle, certain exordia resemble musical preludes, but their essential role in most cases is functional: to win the members of the audience to the speaker's side by creating or fostering among them an atmosphere of interest and good will. When time presses and the speaker is well known to his audience, the exordium can be put aside. To omit it affects the fullness but not the order of the speech. Besides, in our day the purpose of an exordium is often attained by the presiding officer's introduction of the speaker.

The exordium can be about the speaker, the audience, the relevance or importance of the subject, or about the opponent. Aristotle notes in this regard that an exordium which concerns the speaker or his opponent tries to set aside an unfavorable prejudice against the speaker or to create an unfavorable one toward his opponent.[2] But he remarks quite usefully that when it concerns putting aside a prejudice against the speaker it is indispensable to begin the speech with it, because the members of an audience will not listen voluntarily to someone whom they consider hostile or reprehensible; but when it is a matter of crushing the opponent, the arguments must be placed at the end of the speech so that the judges will remember them clearly during the peroration. We see that for Aristotle the place of a development and of an argument is functional: it depends upon the sought-for end and upon the most effective means of reaching it.

It is for this reason that the narration, that is, the exposition of the facts, is indispensable in legal proceedings. It can often be dispensed with in a deliberative speech when past facts are fully known and the future cannot be described. In an epideictic discourse—one which either praises or blames—the narration of facts will be essential or superfluous, as the facts are or are not known to the public. The prosecutor in a trial tries to give the facts a presence which cannot be lost sight of by those who will have to judge them. The counsel for the defense will hardly dwell on the facts unless he opposes his opponent's story, but will emphasize what justifies or excuses them.

Should argumentation itself follow or precede the thesis it is meant to support? Cicero advised different procedures depending upon whether the argument is meant to convince or to arouse the audience. In the first case, there is nothing against announcing at the start the thesis to be proved; in the second, it makes sense to prepare the audience by a preliminary argumentation and to give the thesis at the end.[3]

In what order should arguments be presented? Three orders have been recommended, based on the strength of the arguments: the order of increasing strength, the order of decreasing strength, and the Nestorian order, wherein we begin and end with the strongest arguments, leaving the others in the middle.

The trouble with the order of increasing strength is that beginning with the weakest argument turns off the audience, tarnishes the speaker's image, harms his prestige, and diminishes the attention given to him. The order of decreasing strength ends the speech with the weakest arguments, leaving the listeners with a bad impression, often the last thing they will remember. For this reason most of the classical rhetoricians recommended the Nestorian order.

The trouble with this approach is that it presumes that an argument's forcefulness is constant, regardless of the circumstances in which the argument is presented. But this is not the case. The strength of arguments depends upon the way the arguments are received. If the opponent's argumentation has impressed the audience, it is in the speaker's interest to refute it by beginning with clearing the field, so to speak, before presenting his own arguments. On the contrary, when one speaks first, the refutation of the opponent's eventual arguments never precedes the proof of the thesis defended; there may even be reason *not* to bring them up so as not to give the opponent's arguments a weight or presence which their evocation could only reinforce.

We must not forget that the audience, to the degree that speech is effective, changes with its unfolding development. Some arguments will have various weights depending upon whether certain facts, or particular interpretations of facts, are known. To the degree that the aim of the speech is to persuade an audience, the order of argumentation will be adapted to that purpose: each argument ought to come at the moment at which it can have the greatest impact. But since what persuades one audience does not convince another, the effort of adaptation must always be taken up anew.

Is there an unchangeable order, independent of the audience? It is to a similar inquiry that they are devoted who, on the one hand, extol a *natural* or rational order and, on the other hand, see in a speech only a work of art. In both cases they seek an objective order, determined by scientific or aesthetic considerations.

One way of disregarding the importance of the audience is to be preoccupied with only one type of audience, whose adherence is a guarantee of truth. To Plato, philosophical rhetoric is the one that would convince the gods themselves (*Phaedrus,* 273e), a rhetoric based on truth. It is the same in Descartes' *Discourse on Method,* which continues by radicalizing Agricola's and Ramus' efforts, which questioned whether there does not exist a unique order which compels recognition since it is based on the nature of things, and to which rational discourse ought to conform. To the method of prudence, which is relative to opinion, they opposed the method of doctrine or nature "where that which is naturally more obvious should come first."[4]

Instead of opposing what is more obvious to what is less so, Descartes, taking as a model "the method of geometers," sets himself against traditional rhetoric and dialectic, which are satisfied with probability. Aiming for a certainty beyond opinions, he writes in the first part of the *Discourse on Method*: "Reflecting on the number of different opinions that can be maintained by learned men on a single topic, although only one of these can ever be true, I came to regard as almost false whatever merely looked like the truth."[5] From this follows the first rule of his method: "To accept as true nothing that I did not know to be evidently so;" then the second: "To divide each difficulty I should examine into as many parts as possible, and as would be required the better to solve it." The third rule expressly treats our concern, namely, how "to conduct my thoughts in an orderly fashion, starting with what was simplest and easiest to know, and rising little by little to the knowledge of the most complex, even supposing an order where there is no natural precedence among the objects of knowledge." To this he added a final rule: "To make so complete an enumeration of the links in an argument, and to pass them all so thoroughly under review, that I could be sure I had missed nothing."[6]

There would be no reason to find fault with these rules if Descartes had wished to limit their application to mathematical discourse. However, he makes a daring move which leads him to a controversial philosophy when he ventures to mix typically philosophical imagination with mathematical analyses, by transforming the rules inspired by the geometers into universally applicable ones. The following passage expresses his hopes for a truly rational philosophy.

Those long chains of reasoning, all quite simple and quite easy, which geometers are wont to employ in reaching their most difficult demonstrations, had given me occasion to imagine that all the possible objects of human knowledge were linked together in the same way, and that, if we accepted none as true that was not so in fact, and kept to the right order in deducing one from the other, there was nothng so remote that it could not be reached, nothing so hidden that it could not be discovered.[7]

The aim of philosophy, for Descartes, is the discovery of truth in all things, and its basis is the self-evident truth of "the things we conceive very clearly and distinctly."[8] His method would give birth to a completely new philosophy, a true science wherein we proceed from one self-evident truth to another.

But as long as he had not arrived, through this method, at knowing the truth of all things and in order, he writes that "in order that I might not remain irresolute in my actions while reason obliged me to suspend my judgment, but might continue to live as happily as I could, I devised a provisional morality for myself, composed of only three or four maxims."[9] These maxims derive more from the reasonable than the rational, as characterized by self-evidence, and are so indistinct that he hesitates to state whether their number is three or four. If the first three maxims, concerning moderation, perseverance, and self-mastery (rather than mastery of the world) are of universal applicability, the fourth—that of using his whole life to cultivate reason and to advance in the knowledge of the truth—cannot have the same bearing because he cannot recommend that each man lead a scholarly and philosophical life.

While rhetoricians spoke of a natural order outside of discourse, they were in fact thinking of the chronological order which is suited to narration, the order which relies on customs and tradition and which must be followed so as not to attract attention. In contrast, Descartes adopted a unique order inspired of the geometers, an order which always moves from the simple to the complex. Thus the methodological problem ceased to be the rhetorical one of adaptation to an audience and became instead the scientific one of conformity to the nature of things.

From this perspective, rhetoric (according to the view of
Ramus) no longer aims to convince but to please; at best,
rhetoric makes it easier to accept, through the magic of
words and presentation, truths that are known independently of the art of persuasion. From this point of view a
tendency developed, the premises of which were already to
be found in the Platonic conception of rhetoric: a discourse
was essentially thought of as a work of art, as "a living
creature, having a body of its own and a head and feet."[10]
Equally, in this case, even if the order of a discourse is not
based on ontology but upon an aesthetic—in that it
concerns satisfying the demands of creating such a work—
one is separated from the proper rhetorical order, which is
the order best adapted to any given audience.

Reducing the problems of order to a scientific or aesthetic
methodology separates questions of content from questions
of form and discards the problematic proper to rhetoric: the
adaptation of discourse to the audience. To separate
questions of truth from those concerning adherence is to see
in rhetoric only a simple technique of communication. This
is a view that led to rhetoric's degeneration, and to the
subsequent transformation of ancient rhetoric, a technique
of persuasion, into a rhetoric of figures, purely ornamental
and, at best, literary.

14. The Realm of Rhetoric

THE RELATIONS BETWEEN philosophy and rhetoric have been essential to the destiny of rhetoric. Whereas rhetoric seeks to have certain opinions prevail over other competing opinions, philosophy, which originally included the individual sciences, is seeking impersonal truths. Parmenides began the competition between philosophers and teachers of rhetoric when, in his famous poem, he opposed the way of truth, as guaranteed by divinity, to that of opinion, which is the way of man. Gorgias' reply was not long in coming; he showed, by a three-part argumentation, that Being is not, that if it existed it would be unknowable, and that if it were known this knowledge would be incommunicable. Hence the importance of rhetoric, of the psychological technique which acts upon the hearer's will in order to obtain his adherence. Similarly, by showing that for any subject there are two opposing discourses *(dissoi logoi),* Protagoras denied the existence of one single truth. In this view, every assertion is subject to controversy, since a person can always argue either for or against it. Consequently, preeminence must be granted to the rhetorician, the controller of opinion.

Plato, on the other hand, to the extent that he believed in the existence in every subject area of a truth which the philosopher must seek above all else, recognized a cleansing role in dialectic—the technique Socrates used to refute his opponent's opinions insofar as he was able to bring out their internal inconsistencies. As soon as they contradict themselves, opinions can not be simultaneously admitted, and at least one of them has to be abandoned for the sake of truth. In this way Socrates prepares the way for the intuition of truth. When he has perceived the truth, the philosopher can use rhetorical technique to communicate it and to make his audience accept it. The rhetoric that is worthy of the philosopher can persuade the gods themselves because it seeks acceptance of true theses and not of mere opinions.[1] A rhetoric which neglects truth and is content to get and keep the adherence of the audience through the effects of language, the charm of the word, and a resort to flattery is merely a technique of appearance. Such a rhetoric can be compared to men who, instead of maintaining their bodies by gymnastics and proper medical care, indulge themselves with pleasant food, without concern for the disastrous effects which will result from such gluttony.[2] Rhetoric, seeking to please, concerned only with appearance, and applying "colors," like makeup, to reality, is the demagogic technique *par excellence* which must be combatted by all who are concerned with the triumph of truth. The rhetorician, like the Sophist, is the controller of opinion and hence of appearance, while what matters to the philosopher and the sage is the knowledge of truth and the practice of the good, in conformity to that truth. If dialectic is useful to the philosopher, by allowing him to unsettle erroneous opinions, the perception of truth will come through intuitions; rhetoric will serve to communicate these truths and to gain their acceptance. In this sense, rhetoric is clearly subordinated to philosophy.

Aristotle's conceptions are more nuanced. In separating practical disciplines from theoretical sciences, he stresses the point that the same methods and the same means of proof are not usable in all fields of knowledge. We have already cited the passage from the *Nicomachean Ethics*[3] in which Aristotle shows that what is suitable in a mathematical demonstration would be out of place in a speech, and vice versa.

If it is intuition that guarantees the truth of principles in the theoretical sciences, it is recourse to deliberation and discussion that gives rationality to practical activities, where one is to decide and choose, after reflection, among possibilities and contingencies. Through dialectical reasoning and rhetoric, one can influence people's judgment and direct them toward taking reasonable positions. In Aristotle's view, every audience is a judge which in the end must decide the superiority of one disputed thesis over the other when neither is obviously compelling. Since the realm of action is the realm of the contingent, which cannot be governed by scientific truths, the role of dialectical reasoning and rhetorical discourse is essential in order to introduce some rationality into the exercise of the individual and the collective will.

We showed in chapter one how Ramus attributed to dialectic the study of every kind of reasoning, analytical as well as dialectical, and thus reduced rhetoric to elocution, the search for forms of expression that were out of the ordinary, for ornamentation, for figures of style. But Descartes went even further in his desire to eliminate all rhetoric from his philosophy.[5] His idea of a philosophy *more geometrico* (which was not realized until Spinoza) was to build a system which, moving from one self-evidence to another, would leave no room for any disputable opinion. As Descartes puts it at the beginning of his *First Meditation:*

> Since reason already convinces me that I should abstain from the belief in things which are not entirely certain and indubitable no less carefully than from the belief in those which appear to me to be manifestly false, it will be enough to make me reject them all if I can find in each some ground for doubt.[6]

The attempt to elaborate a philosophy wherein all theses would be either self-evident or compellingly demonstrated leads to the elimination of all forms of argumentation and to the rejection of rhetoric as an instrument of philosophy.

What are the presuppositions of such a philosophy? In the first place there is the idea that God is not only the source but also the guarantor of all knowledge, because "I must examine whether there is a God, and . . . whether he can be a deceiver; for as long as this is unknown, I do not see that I can ever be certain of anything."[7] Descartes' method is to discover "a path that will lead us from this contemplation of the true God, in whom all the treasures of science and wisdom are contained, to the knowledge of all other beings."[8]

Scientific knowledge is wholly complete; all we have to do is recover it.

It is necessary to be suspicious of all human initiative, which can only lead to error, since it arises from imagination and prejudice. Human creativity, in scientific work, is completely neglected.

Divine ideas, being completely rational, can only be mathematical. They alone are characterized by self-evidence, which compels every rational being to submit to it. Because of Descartes' philosophic imagination, he generalized the results of the analysis of mathematical reasoning; he required (contrary to Aristotle's advice) that the same demands for rigor which had succeeded so well in mathematics be applied to all other realms. This led him to a methodological doubt concerning opinion:

> As far as the opinions which I had been receiving since my birth were concerned, I could not do better than to reject them completely for once in my lifetime, and to resume them afterwards, or perhaps accept better ones in their place, when I had determined how they fitted in a rational scheme.[9]

Many years previously, Lord Bacon, theoretician of the empirical sciences, had also preached Christian humility to the learned, asking them to read carefully the book of nature, by which God revealed himself to man. The inductive method should guard man from formulating any thesis which could not be found in the book of nature, as if all experience had been clearly described in a divine language.

Having noted the theological background of the conception of science, both with Bacon and with Descartes, and having underscored the paradoxical and hardly admissable aspect of the Cartesian imagination, which would subject all opinions to the same criterion of self-evidence as mathematical theses, we should point out that even Descartes had to trust opinions for his provisional morality. Before reconstructing a rational science, he had to accept a provisional morality and its maxims. The first of these was "to obey the laws and customs of my country, constantly retaining the religion in which, by God's grace, I had been brought up since childhood, and in all other matters to follow the most moderate and least excessive opinions to be found in the practices of the more judicious part of the community in which I would live."[10]

We know that in the course of his life Descartes had to be satisfied with his provisional morality. His concern for generalized self-evidence did not result in the replacement of traditional morality—the expression of the common opinion of his milieu—by a rational, universally valid morality. Rather, it caused him to respect the ruling opinions and regulations scrupulously, and he refused to modify them for any nonself-evident reason. Paradoxically, mathematical rationalism, which went with a rejection of all opinion, of every exchange of opinions, of every recourse to dialectic and rhetoric, led finally to immobility and conformism in law, morality, politics, and religion.

Even today the teaching of the sciences is inspired by the Cartesian approach. In the areas which are free from controversy, it is not customary to refer to the opinion of one or another scholar. The theses which are taught are considered true, or are accepted as hypotheses; but there is hardly any need to justify them.

Thus, although axioms in the mathematical sciences, considered at first self-evident, were subsequently shown to be conventions of language, this change of perspective, however fundamental, has not affected the way in which such formal systems are laid out. In fact, if it is not a question of self-evidence, but of hypotheses or conventions, why choose this hypothesis or that convention rather than another? Most mathemeticians consider such questions foreign to their discipline.

When, under the influence of mathematicians, logic was presented in the form of several formalized systems, logicians with philosophical concerns asked if it were necessary to admit several different kinds of logic, or if a single, natural logic, prior to all formalized systems, existed. If there is a natural logic, how is it to be disengaged from other systems? Would it be drawn from the very structure of natural language?[11] Would it be justified by the needs of a methodological discussion?[12] As soon as we pose the problem of a choice of logic and its justification, an impersonal science leads us back to its philosophical and properly human foundations.

Likewise, the natural sciences were for centuries able to do without reference to a human language, situated in a historical and cultural context, by referring to God, to his ideas, and to the manner by which he revealed them to man. Belief in the existence of eternal truths, contained in the divine mind and guaranteed by it, justified the elimination of all personal elements from scientific thought, error alone being attributable to human intervention.

Take away the guarantee which God gives to self-evidence and, suddenly, all thought becomes human and fallible, and no longer sheltered from controversy. The idea that any scientific theory is only a human hypothesis, necessarily surpassing, if it would be fruitful, the data given by experience, and being neither self-evident nor infallible, is a modern conception which Karl Popper has effectively defended.[13] But, lacking the self-evidence that can be imposed on everyone, a hypothesis, to be accepted, must be supported by good reasons, recognized as such by other people, members of the same scientific community. The status of knowledge thus ceases to be impersonal because every scientific thought becomes a human one, i.e., fallible, situated in and subjected to controversy. Every new idea must be supported by arguments which are relevant to its discipline's proper methodology and which are evaluated in terms of it.

The Cartesian ideal of universally applicable self-evident knowledge leaves no room for rhetoric and dialectic. Their importance increases, however, each time a field of knowledge is no longer dominated by the criterion of self-evidence. A critique of the idea of self-evidence,[14] showing that it vanishes as soon as it is necessary to go beyond subjective intuition—as soon as one wishes to communicate it through a language which is never compelling—tends to show that the choice of a mode of expression, if it is not arbitrary—and it rarely is—is influenced by reasons which come from dialectic and rhetoric. All intellectual activity which is placed between the necessary and the arbitrary is reasonable only to the degree that it is maintained by arguments and eventually clarified by controversies which normally do not lead to unanimity.

Indeed, it happens that, coming to an agreement on a methodology, people can obtain in certain periods and in certain disciplines a unanimity which they may not find again elsewhere; but nothing guarantees its indefinite continuation. Even the Newtonian formula of universal attraction, which was believed to be unshakable, was breached when people were given sufficient reasons to modify it.

Contrary to Descartes, who wanted to build all knowledge on unshakable self-evidence, we must show that the consensus of scientists, based on specific lines of reasoning, is the exception.

In all other fields, whether religion or philosophy, ethics or law, pluralism is the rule. These fields draw their rationality only from the argumentative apparatus, from good reasons which can be offered for or against each presented thesis.

Since Hegel, it is hard to deny that any philosophy is both historically situated and subject to controversy. And this affirmation applies to the Hegelian system itself as soon as it is detached from its theological underpinnings. This implies putting classical epistemology and metaphysics into question. Instead of searching for a necessary and self-evident first truth from which all our knowledge would be suspended, let us recast our philosophy in terms of a vision in which people and human societies are in interaction and are solely responsible for their cultures, their institutions, and their future—a vision in which people try hard to elaborate reasonable systems, imperfect but perfectible.

The preeminent realm of argumentation, dialectic, and rhetoric is that in which values come into play. Plato, in his dialogue on piety (the *Euthyphro*) had shown that the privileged realm of dialectic is the one which transcends calculation, weight, and measure, the one in which we deal with the just and the unjust, the beautiful and the ugly, the good and the bad, and in general, with the preferable.[15]

The modern conception of philosophy, which distinguishes it from the sciences, considers argumentation in all its forms as the method proper to philosophy.

Indeed, philosophy cannot be limited to what is perceived, for its proper task is to separate the important from the secondary, the essential from the accidental, the construct from the given, all from a perspective whose pertinence and superiority does not compel everyone. Hence the obligation to support the chosen perspective through argumentation, using analogies and metaphors, by which the adequacy and superiority of the one perspective over rival perspectives can be shown.

It is clear that the philosopher's forms of reasoning cannot be limited to deduction and induction. To the extent that philosophers appeal to reason and use, to win over an audience, a whole arsenal of arguments which ought to be accepted by everyone, just so must they broaden their conception of reason so as to demonstrate the rationality of argumentative techniques and rhetoric, as a theory of persuasive discourse.

We will be helped in this enterprise, inescapable in our time, by the secular experience of the jurists, who, having made human institutions depend upon a natural law of divine inspiration—be it the providence of the Stoics, the living God of the revealed religions, or the rational God of the philosophers—later came to elaborate a theory of "a reasonable law," an object of the consensus of an organized community.[16]

Understandably, treatises on rhetoric in antiquity were esentially works for the use of jurists. But we must not forget in this regard that law, unlike philosophy for example, aims at settling disputes which cannot be prolonged indefinitely. In law a decision must be reached which takes advantage of the authority of legal precedent.[17]

Philosophical, like juridical, argumentation constitutes the application to particular fields of a general theory of argumentation which we understand as a new rhetoric. In identifying this rhetoric with the general theory of persuasive discourse, which seeks to gain both the intellectual and the emotional adherence of any sort of audience, we affirm that every discourse which does not claim an impersonal validity belongs to rhetoric. As soon as a communication tries to influence one or more persons, to orient their thinking, to excite or calm their emotions, to guide their actions, it belongs to the realm of rhetoric. Dialectic, the technique of controversy, is included as one part of this larger realm.

Thus rhetoric covers the vast field of nonformalized thought: we can thus speak of "the realm of rhetoric."[18] It is in this spirit that Professor Jens of the University of Tübingen described rhetoric as "the once and future queen of the human sciences" [*alte und neue Königin der Wissenschaften*].[19]

Rhetoric, conceived as the theory of persuasive communication, has aroused growing interest among scholars and philosophers. Things have changed in the last thirty years. Not so long ago, rhetoric was disdained in Europe. In the United States, where speech departments were numerous,[20] they were hardly held in esteem by the academic community. Today rhetoric is rehabilitated, contrary to the opinion of the well-known historian Jacob Burckhart, who had called it "a monstrous aberration" of Greco-Roman antiquity.

Notes

Introduction

1. *L'Empire rhétorique,* "Preface," p. 9. For this account see also Ch. Perelman, "The New Rhetoric: A Theory of Practical Reasoning," *The Great Ideas of Today: 1970* (Chicago: Encyclopaedia Britannica, 1970), pp. 271-312; a historical sketch appears on pp. 280-281.

2. Aristotle *Topics* (Trans. E.S. Forster) 100a, 18-21.

3. Three randomly chosen modern works illustrate contemporary uncertainty concerning how argumentative discourse is to be understood. All three books emulate the theory of formal logic in identifying induction and deduction as the paradigmatic forms of reasoned discourse. On the other hand, the authors of all three books reject the notion that the *rules* of formal logic apply to rhetorical communication. See William J. Brandt, *The Rhetoric of Argumentation* (Indianapolis: Bobbs-Merrill, 1970), p. 212; Martin P. Andersen, E. Ray Nichols, Jr., and Herbert W. Booth, *The Speaker and His Audience* (New York: Harper & Row, 1974, 2nd ed.), p. 398; Charles S. Mudd and Malcolm O. Sillars, *Speech: Content and Communication* (New York: Thomas Y. Crowell, 1975, 3rd. ed.), p. 152.

4. See for example Robert Price, "Some Antistrophes to the *Rhetoric*," *Philosophy & Rhetoric* 1 (Summer 1968), 145-164; esp. pp. 159-160.

5. Perelman and Olbrechts-Tyteca, *The New Rhetoric* (Notre Dame: University of Notre Dame Press, 1969), p. 5.

6. An excellent, recent survey of this conflict is Samuel Ijsseling, *Rhetoric and Philosophy in Conflict* (The Hague: Martinus Nijhoff, 1976).

7. Perelman's conception of philosophical argument came under debate in philosophical literature when it appeared in Ch. Perelman and L. Olbrechts-Tyteca, *Rhétorique et philosophie: Pour une théorie de l'argumentation en philosophie* (Paris: Presses Universitaires de France, 1952).

1. Logic, Dialectic, Philosophy, and Rhetoric

1. "L'ancienne rhétorique, aide-memoire," *Communications* 16 (Paris: Éditions du Seuil, 1970), 194.

2. Aristotle *Topics* 100a, 30-31.

3. *Topics* (ed. Ross, trans. Pickard-Cambridge) 100b, 20-24.

4. Aristotle *Rhetoric* 1356b, 28.

5. Aristotle *Nichomachean Ethics* 1094b, 25-28.

6. Peter Ramus [Pierre de la Ramée], *Dialectique* (1555), ed. M. Dassonville (Geneva: Librairie Droz, 1964), p. 61. See also Dudley Fenner, *The Arts of Logike and Rethorike* (1584), in Robert D. Pepper (ed.), *Four Tudor Books on Education* (Gainesville, Fla.: Scholars' Facsimiles & Reprints, 1966). Fenner's work is a translation of the main heads of Ramus' *Dialecticae libri duo* and of Talon's *Rhetoricae libri duo*.

7. Ibid., p. 50.

8. Ibid., p. 25; cited from the Preface of his *Scholae in liberales artes*.

9. Ibid., p. 62.

10. Fenner, *The Arts of Logike and Rethorike*, in *Four Tudor Books on Education*, p. 171. Cf. Omer Talon, *Rhetoricae libri duo* (1572), p. 16.

11. *Rhetoric* 1354a, 1.

12. *Rhetoric* 1357a.

13. See Perelman, *Logique juridique* (Paris: Dalloz, 1979).

14. See "Self-Evidence and Proof," in Perelman, *The Idea of Justice and the Problem of Argument* (London: Routledge & Kegan Paul, 1963), pp. 109-125, and "De l'évidence en métaphysique," in Perelman, *Le Champ de l'argumentation* (Brussels: Presses Universitaires de Bruxelles, 1970), pp. 236-248.

15. *Topics* 101a and b.

16. See Perelman, "Philosophie, rhétorique, lieux communs," *Bulletin de l'Académie Royale de Belgique* (1972) 144-156; published in English in *The New Rhetoric and the Humanities* (Dordrecht: Reidel, 1979), pp. 52-61.

17. See Perelman, "Analogie et métaphore en science, poésie, et philosophie," *Le Champ de l'argumentation,* pp. 271-286; in English in *The New Rhetoric and the Humanities,* pp. 91-100.

18. See Paul Ricoeur, *The Rule of Metaphor,* trans. Robert Czerny, with Kathleen McGloughlin and John Costello (Toronto: University of Toronto Press, 1977), pp. 247-256.

19. See Perelman and Olbrechts-Tyteca, "Logique et rhétorique," *Rhétorique et philosophie* (Paris: Presses Universitaires de France, 1952), p. 80. See also Roland Barthes, "L'ancienne rhétorique," *Communications,* p. 192.

20. See R. Blanché, *Le Raisonnement* (Paris: Presses Universitaires de France, 1973), pp. 230-231, and also M. Villey, "Nouvelle rhétorique et droit naturel," *Logique et analyse* 73 (1976) 4-10.

2. *Argumentation, Speaker, and Audience*

1. *Topics* 101a and b.

2. *Topics* 105a.

3. Demosthenes *First Olynthiac* 19.

4. Pascal, *Pensées,* trans. W.F. Trotter (New York: Modern Library, 1941), 417.

5. St. Augustine, *On Christian Doctrine,* 4, 13, trans. D.W. Robertson, Jr. (New York: Liberal Arts Press, 1958), p. 138.

6. Ibid., pp. 136-137.

7. *Pensées,* 260. See *The New Rhetoric,* p. 40.

8. Descartes, *Meditations on First Philosophy,* trans. Laurence J. Lafleur (Indianapolis: Bobbs-Merrill, 1960), p. 11.

9. See *The New Rhetoric,* p. 41.

10. Anthelme Edouard Chaignet, *La Rhétorique et son histoire* (Paris: E. Bouillon et E. Vieweg, 1888), p. 93.

11. Arthur Schopenhauer, "On Ethics," *Parerga and Paralepomena: Short Philosophical Essays,* trans. E.F.J. Payne (Oxford: Clarendon Press, 1974), II, 234. See *The New Rhetoric,* p. 42.

12. Quintilian *Institutio oratorio* 2. 20. 7.

13. See Michael Polanyi, *Personal Knowledge* (London: Routledge and Kegan Paul, 1958), pp. 292-294.

14. See Thomas Kuhn, *The Structure of Scientific Revolutions* (Chicago: University of Chicago Press, 1970).

15. See Pascal, *Pensées,* 252.

16. See Immanuel Kant, *Critique of Pure Reason,* trans. N.K. Smith (New York: St. Martin's Press, 1961), pp. 626-627.

17. See *The New Rhetoric,* pp. 26-45.

18. *Rhetoric* 1389-1391.

19. *Rhetoric* (trans. Freese) 1358b, 2-7.

20. *Rhetoric* 1358b, 28.

21. *The New Rhetoric,* p. 48.

3. The Premises of Argumentation

1. See Octave Navarre, *Essai sur la rhétorique grecque avant Aristote* (Paris: Hachette, 1900), p. 141, note 1. See *The New Rhetoric,* p. 113.

2. Jeremy Bentham, *Works* (Edinburgh: W. Tait, 1843), II: *The Book of Fallacies,* p. 436.

3. Henri Poincaré, *The Value of Science,* trans. George Bruce Halsted (New York: Dover, 1958), p. 14.

4. *The New Rhetoric,* p. 67.

5. Ludwig Wittgenstein, *On Certainty* (Oxford: Blackwell, 1969).

6. Cf. Michael Polanyi, *Personal Knowledge* (Chicago: University of Chicago Press, 1958), Part III, "The Justification of Personal Knowledge."

7. *The New Rhetoric,* pp. 70-71.

8. See *Les Présomptions et les fictions en droit,* studies published by Ch. Perelman (Brussels: Bruylant, 1974), pp. 340-341.

9. Louis Lavelle, *Traité des valeurs* (Paris: Presses Universitaires de France, 1951), I, 13.

10. Eugene Dupréel, *Sociologie générale* (Paris: Presses Universitaires de France, 1948), pp. 181-182.

11. *The New Rhetoric*, p. 77.

12. *Discourse on Method*, trans. Laurence J. Lafleur (New York: The Liberal Arts Press, 1956), pp. 22-23.

13. Scheler, *Formalism in Ethics and Non-Formal Ethics of Values*, trans. Manfred S. Frings and Roger L. Funk (Evanston: Northwestern University Press, 1973), pp. 85-86.

14. *Rhetoric* 1358a.

15. *Rhetoric* 1362a-1365b, *Topics* 116a-119a.

16. See "Classicisme et romanticisme dans l'argumentation," *Le Champ de l'argumentation*, pp. 397-406. English version in *The New Rhetoric and the Humanities*, pp. 159-167.

17. Marcel Proust, *The Guermantes Way*, trans. C.K. Scott Moncrieff (New York: Modern Library, 1925), pt. II, p. 181.

18. *Pensées*, 216.

19. Plato *Gorgias* (trans. W.D. Woodhead) 487d-e.

20. Ibid.

4. Choice, Presence, and Presentation

1. See Perelman, "A Propos de l'objectivité de l'information," *Publics et techniques de la diffusion collective* (Editions de l'Université de Bruxelles, 1970), pp. 81-88.

2. *Critique of Pure Reason*, pp. 645-646.

3. *Gorgias* 487d-e.

4. Cited in Pauthier, *Confucius et Mencius* (Paris: Charpentier, 1852), I, § 7. See *The New Rhetoric*, p. 116.

5. Francis Bacon, *Advancement of Learning* (London: Oxford University Press, 1944), I, 156-157.

6. Arthur Koestler *et al*, *The God That Failed*, ed. Richard H. Crossman (London: Hamilton, 1950), pp. 253-254. See *The New Rhetoric*, pp. 118-119.

7. Richard M. Weaver, "Language is Sermonic," *Contemporary Theories of Rhetoric*, ed. R. Johannesen (New York: Harper & Row, 1971), p. 173.

8. *Rhetoric* 1357a.

9. *The New Rhetoric*, p. 144.

10. See Vico, *Delle instituzioni oratorie, Opere,* Vol. VII (Naples, 1865), p. 87.

11. Fléchier, *Oraison funèbre de Henri de La Tour d'Auvergne, vicomte de Turenne;* cited in *The New Rhetoric,* p. 145.

12. Vico, *Delle instituzioni oratorie,* p. 81, cited in *The New Rhetoric,* p. 176.

13. Corneille, *The Cid,* 1, 6; cited in *The New Rhetoric,* p. 176.

14. *Rhetorica ad Herennium* 4, 68; cited in *The New Rhetoric,* p. 167.

15. See Sartre, *Being and Nothingness,* trans. H.E. Barnes (New York: Philosophical Library, 1956), p. 135.

16. Longinus *On the Sublime* 15. See *The New Rhetoric,* p. 171.

17. See *The New Rhetoric,* p. 152.

5. Significance and Interpretation of Data

1. Ernest Gellner, "Maxims," *Mind* 60, new series, 1951, p. 393. See *The New Rhetoric,* p. 121.

2. Locke, *An Essay Concerning Human Understanding,* ed. Peter H. Nidditch (Oxford: The Clarendon Press, 1975), III, ix, 9, p. 480.

3. See *The New Rhetoric,* p. 123.

4. I.A. Richards, *The Philosophy of Rhetoric* (London: Oxford University Press, 1936), p. 3.

5. See Ricoeur, *The Rule of Metaphor,* pp. 138-143.

6. See Ch. Perelman, "Perspectives rhétoriques sur les problèmes sémantiques," *Logique et Analyse,* 1974, pp. 241-252. English version in *The New Rhetoric,* pp. 82-90.

7. *Pensées,* 686. See *The New Rhetoric,* p. 124.

8. See Jean Cohen, *Structure du langage poétique* (Paris: Flammarion, 1966), pp. 45, 51, 114, 117, 182.

9. *Rhetoric* 1405b.

10. André Gide, *Prétextes* (Paris: Mercure de France, 1947), p. 135.

11. Ibid., p. 175. See *The New Rhetoric,* p. 129.

12. C. Gal. 306b. Quoted in Joseph Bidez, *La Vie de l'empereur Julien* (Paris: Société d'édition "Les Belles Lettres," 1930), p. 305. See *The New Rhetoric,* p. 157.

13. See *The New Rhetoric*, pp. 154-163.

6. *Techniques of Argumentation*

1. Jacques-Bénigne Bossuet, *Sermons* (Paris: Garnier, 1942), II, "Sur l'impénitence finale." Cited in *The New Rhetoric*, p. 191.

2. See *The New Rhetoric*, pp. 191-192.

3. *Institutio oratorio* 5, 10, 67. See *The New Rhetoric*, p. 235.

4. Bossuet, *Sermons*, II, "Sur la parole de Dieu." Cited in *The New Rhetoric*, p. 261.

5. See Ch. Perelman, "Le Réel commun et le réel philosophique," *Le Champ de l'argumentation*, pp. 253-264.

7. *Quasi-Logical Arguments*

1. See *The New Rhetoric*, on the role of the ridiculous, pp. 205-210.

2. L. Olbrechts-Tyteca, *Le Comique du discours* (Brussels: Editions de l'Université de Bruxelles, 1974), p. 160.

3. Isocrates *Busiris* 26. See *The New Rhetoric*, p. 209.

4. La Bruyère, "Les Caractères, Des femmes," 50, *Oeuvres complètes* (Paris: Bibliotheque de la Pléiade, 1951), p. 142.

5. *The New Rhetoric*, p. 202.

6. G. Isaye, "La Justification critique par rétorsion," *Revue Philosophique de Louvain*, 1954, pp. 205-233.

7. *The New Rhetoric*, p. 204.

8. L. Olbrechts-Tyteca, *Le Comique du discours*, pp. 169-173.

9. Ibid., p. 172.

10. Epictetus *Discourses* (trans. Matheson) 1. 23. See *The New Rhetoric*, p. 205.

11. Proust, *The Guermantes Way*, trans. C.K. Scott Moncrieff (New York: Modern Library), II, 176-177. See *The New Rhetoric*, p. 198.

12. Vladimir Jankelevitch, *Traité des vertus* (Paris: Bordas, 1949), p. 435. See *The New Rhetoric*, p. 199.

13. Arne Naess, *Interpretation and Preciseness: A Contribution to the Theory of Communication* (Oslo: J. Dybwad, 1953), ch. 4. See *The New Rhetoric,* pp. 210-211.

14. Perelman, *The Idea of Justice and the Problem of Argument* (London: Routledge and Kegan Paul, 1963), pp. 2-3.

15. John Wisdom, "Logical Constructions," *Mind* 40-41 (1931-33). See *The New Rhetoric,* pp. 214-215.

16. L.S. Stebbing, "The Method of Analysis in Metaphysics," *Proceedings of the Aristotelian Society* 33 (1932-33), pp. 65-94.

17. P.F. Strawson, *Introduction to Logical Theory* (London: Methuen, 1952), ch. 6, III, par. 7.

18. *The New Rhetoric,* p. 217.

19. Jouhandeau, *Ana de Madame Apremont,* (Paris, 1954), p. 61. Also Ch. Perelman, "Perspectives rhétoriques sur les problemes semantiques," *Logique et analyse,* 1974, p. 244.

20. See *The New Rhetoric,* pp. 216-217.

21. G. Frege, "Über Sinn und Bedeutung," *Zeitschrift für Philosophische Kritik,* 100 (1892), 25-50. See also Perelman, *Justice* (New York: Random House, 1967), pp. 21-22.

22. Perelman, *The Idea of Justice and the Problem of Argument,* p. 15.

23. Demosthenes *On the Treaty with Alexander* par. 18.

24. C. Virgil Gheorghiu, *The Twenty-Fifth Hour* (New York: Alfred A. Knopf, 1950), pp. 276-277.

25. Locke, *The Second Treatise on Civil Government and a Letter Concerning Toleration* (Oxford: B. Blackwell, 1948), p. 136.

26. Quintilian *Institutio oratoria* 5. 10. 78.

27. *Rhetoric* 1397a, 25.

28. La Bruyère, "Les Caractères, De quelques usages," 21, p. 432.

29. L. Olbrechts-Tyteca, *Le Comique du discours,* p. 199.

30. Isocrates *Panegyric of Athens* 81.

31. L. Olbrechts-Tyteca, *Le Comique du discours,* p. 200.

32. Sterne, *The Life and Opinions of Tristram Shandy, Gentleman,* ed. James Aiken Work (Indianapolis: The Odyssey Press, 1940), Vol. IV, ch. 29, p. 330-331.

33. Jouhandeau, *Un monde* (Paris: Gallimard, 1950), p. 25. See *The New Rhetoric,* pp. 226-227.

34. Montaigne, *Essays,* I, 20, *The Complete Works of Montaigne,* trans. Donald M. Frame (Stanford: Stanford University Press, 1957), p. 64.

35. The *Ta Hio,* I, 4. In *The Sacred Books of the East,* ed. F. Max Miller, trans. J. Legge (Oxford: Clarendon Press, 1879), Vol. 28, pp. 411-412. See *The New Rhetoric,* pp. 230-231.

36. Locke, *A Letter Concerning Toleration,* p. 135.

37. *Traité des vertus,* p. 19.

38. *The New Rhetoric,* p. 234.

39. L. Olbrechts-Tyteca, *Le Comique du discours,* p. 208.

40. Locke, *A Letter Concerning Toleration,* p. 136.

41. Demosthenes *First Olynthiac* pars. 25, 27.

42. André Vayson de Pradennes, *Les Fraudes en archéologie préhistorique* (Paris: E. Nourry, 1932), p. 533. See *The New Rhetoric,* p. 237.

43. *Tristram Shandy,* Vol. IV, "Slawkenbergius' Tale," pp. 259-260.

44. Cicero, *De oratore* 2. 172.

45. Bossuet, *Sermons,* II, "Sur l'ambition," p. 395. See *The New Rhetoric,* p. 244.

46. *Enneads* (trans. MacKenna and Page) 6. 8. 8.

47. La Bruyère, "Les Caracteres, du mérite personnel," 25, p. 118.

48. *The New Rhetoric,* pp. 244-245.

49. *Pensées,* 397.

50. Calvin, *Institutes of the Christian Religion* (London: Westminster Press, 1960), I, 16.

51. *Enneads* 6. 7. 34.

52. Simone Weil, *The Need for Roots,* trans. Arthur Wills (New York: Putnam, 1952), p. 129. See *The New Rhetoric,* p. 250.

53. Jean Paulhan, *Le Guerrier appliqué* (Paris: Gallimard, 1930), p. 133.

54. L. Olbrechts-Tyteca, *Le Comique du discours,* p. 219.

55. Isocrates *Archidamus* 4. See *The New Rhetoric,* p. 256.

56. *A Letter Concerning Toleration,* p. 128.

57. *Pensées,* 233.

8. Arguments Based on the Structure of Reality

1. *The New Rhetoric*, pp. 263-292.

2. Ibid., pp. 293-349.

3. Perelman, "Pragmatic Arguments," *The Idea of Justice and the Problem of Argument*, pp. 196-207. See *The New Rhetoric*, pp. 266-270.

4. Bentham, *The Theory of Legislation*, ed. C.K. Odgen (London: Routledge and Kegan Paul, 1931), pp. 66-67.

5. Charles Odier, M.D. *Anxiety and Magical Thinking*, trans. Marie-Louise Schoelly and Mary Jane Sherberg (New York: International Universities Press, 1956), p. 147.

6. Max Scheler, *The Formalism of Ethics and the Ethics of Non-Formal Values*, p. 221.

7. Simone Weil, *The Need for Roots*, p. 251. *See also* Perelman, "Pragmatic Arguments," *The Idea of Justice*, p. 206.

8. Cicero, *Paradoxa Stoicorum* 4. 29. See *The New Rhetoric*, p. 273.

9. Charles Lalo, *Esthétique du rire* (Paris: Flammarion, 1949), p. 159. See *The New Rhetoric*, p. 272.

10. Cf. L. Olbrechts-Tyteca, *Le Comique du discours*, p. 240.

11. Proust, *The Captive*, trans. C.K. Scott Moncrieff (New York: Modern Library, 1941), pp. 505-506.

12. Edmond Goblot, *La Logique des jugements de valeur* (Paris: A. Colin, 1927), pp. 55-56.

13. Isocrates *Panegyric of Athens* 84. See *The New Rhetoric*, p. 252.

14. L. Olbrechts-Tyteca, *Le Comique du discours*, p. 240.

15. Ibid., p. 242.

16. Bossuet, *Sermons*, II, "Sur la compassion de la Sainte Vierge," p. 645, "Sur la pénitence," p. 72.

17. *The New Rhetoric*, p. 281.

18. Bentham, *Works*, Vol. II, *The Book of Fallacies*, Part III, "Fallacies of Delay," p. 433.

19. Ibid.

20. *The New Rhetoric*, pp. 290-292.

21. *The New Rhetoric*, p. 294.

22. Burke, *A Grammar of Motives* (New York: George Braziller, 1945), p. 42.

23. Perelman and Olbrechts-Tyteca, "Act and Person in Argument," *The Idea of Justice and the Problem of Argument,* pp. 168-195.

24. S.E. Asch, "The Doctrine of Suggestion, Prestige, and Imitation in Social Psychology," *Psychology Review* 5 (1948), pp. 250-276.

25. Calvin, *Institutes,* I, ch. 18.

26. André Lalande, *La Raison et ses normes* (Paris: Hachette, 1948), p. 196. See *The New Rhetoric,* p. 302.

27. Dupréel, *Sociologie générale,* p. 66.

28. Baltasar Gracian, *L'homme de Cour* [*Oráculo manual y arte de prudencia*], French translation by the Sieur Amelot de la Houssaie (Augsburg: Paul Kühtze, 1710), p. 217. See *The New Rhetoric,* p. 303.

29. *The New Rhetoric,* p. 307.

30. Bossuet, *Sermons,* II, "Sur la soumission due à la parole de Jésus-Christ," pp. 117-121.

31. Leibniz, *Theodicy: Essays on the Goodness of God, the Freedom of Man, and the Origin of Evil,* ed. Austin Farrer, trans. E.M. Huggard (London: Routledge & Kegan Paul, 1951), p. 98.

32. Bossuet, *Sermons,* II, "Sur les vaines excuses des pécheurs," p. 489. See *The New Rhetoric,* p. 316.

33. *Rhetoric* 1416a.

34. *Rhetoric* 1356a.

35. *Les Catégories en histoire,* ed. Chaim Perelman (Brussels, 1969).

36. Aristotle *Topics* 116b.

37. Leibniz, *Discourse on Metaphysics,* 37, *Leibniz: Selections,* ed. Philip P. Weiner (New York: Charles Scribner's Sons, 1951), p. 344.

38. Aristotle *Topics* 116b, 10-15.

39. Sophocles *Antigone.*

40. Plato *Phaedrus* 247d-248b.

41. Plotinus *Enneads* 6. 9. 3.

42. *The New Rhetoric,* p. 345.

43. Montaigne, *Essays,* I, 20.

44. Bossuet, *Sermons,* II, "Sur l'honneur."

45. Cicero *Paradoxa stoicorum* 3. 20. See *The New Rhetoric,* p. 345.

9. Argumentation by Example, Illustration, and Method

1. L. Olbrechts-Tyteca, *Le Comique du discours*, p. 280.
2. Roger Caillois, *Poétique de St.-John Perse* (Paris: Gallimard, 1954), p. 152.
3. *Rhetoric* 1393b.
4. *Rhetoric* 1398b.
5. Karl Popper, *The Logic of Scientific Discovery* (London: Hutchinson, 1959).
6. Descartes, *Discourse on Method*, pp. 44-45.
7. Ibid., p. 45.
8. Epictetus *Discourses* 1, 24. See *The New Rhetoric*, p. 361.
9. Plato, *The Republic* 488b-489d.
10. Shakespeare, *Julius Caesar*, act 3, scene 2.
11. Isocrates *To Nicocles* 31. See *The New Rhetoric*, p. 363.
12. Pascal, *Pensées*, 103.
13. Montaigne, *Essays*, III, 20, p. 703.
14. Méré, *Oeuvres complètes* (Paris: F. Roches, 1930), Vol. II, pp. 30-31. See *The New Rhetoric*, pp. 366-367.
15. Bossuet, *Sermons*, vol. II, p. 50.
16. Ibid., p. 411.
17. Locke, *A Letter Concerning Toleration*, p. 139.
18. S. Weil, *The Need for Roots*, p. 90.

10. Analogy and Metaphor

1. Epictetus *Discourses* 3. 9. See *The New Rhetoric*, p. 381.
2. Leibniz, *Discourse on Metaphysics*, 32, in *Philosophical Writings*, p. 41.
3. Joannes Scotus Erigena, *De divina praedestinatione* 4. 8.
4. Diels, *Fragments*, 79. See *The New Rhetoric*, p. 375.
5. Calvin, *Institutes*, pp. 26-27. See *The New Rhetoric*, p. 378.
6. Sterne, *Tristam Shandy*, Vol. VIII, ch. 19, p. 568.
7. Louis Réau, "L'influence de la forme sur l'iconographie médiévale," *Formes de l'art, formes de l'esprit* (Paris: Presses Universitaires de France, 1951), pp. 91-92. See *The New Rhetoric*, p. 379.

8. Bossuet, *Oraisons funébres*, p. 218. See *The New Rhetoric*, p. 379.

9. Quintilian *Institutio oratoria* 8. 3. 76. See *The New Rhetoric*, p. 380.

10. La Bruyère, "Les Caractères, De la Cour," 65 *Oeuvres complètes*, p. 257. See *The New Rhetoric*, p. 386.

11. Kant, *Prolegomena to Any Future Metaphysics*, trans. Paul Carus (Chicago: Open Court, 1902), p. 9.

12. M. Black, *Models and Metaphors* (Ithaca: Cornell University Press, 1962), pp. 42-45.

13. Willis Moore, "Structure in Sentence and in Fact," *Philosophy of Science*, 5 (1938), p. 87.

14. Leibniz, "Preface," to *New Essays on the Human Understanding*, in *Philosophical Writings*, ed. G.H.R. Harrison, trans. Mary Morris and G.H.R. Parkinson (London: J.M. Dent & Sons, 1973), p. 153. See *The New Rhetoric*, p. 389.

15. Michael Polanyi, *The Logic of Liberty* (London: Routledge and Kegan Paul, 1951), pp. 87-89.

16. *Poetics* (trans. W.H. Fyfe) 1457b.

17. Perelman, *Le Champ de l'argumentation*, p. 274.

18. Ronsard, "A sa maîtresse," Ode XVII, *Oeuvres complètes*, ed. La Pléiade, Vol. I, pp. 419-420. English translation from *Songs and Sonnets of Pierre de Ronsard*, trans. Curtis Hidden Page (Westport, CT: Hyperion, 1978), p. 67.

19. L. Olbrechts-Tyteca, *Le Comique du discours*, p. 307.

20. Descartes, *Rules for the Direction of the Mind*, trans. L.J. Lafleur (Indianapolis: Bobbs-Merrill, 1961), pp. 25-26.

21. Perelman, *Le Champ de l'argumentation*, p. 277.

22. Descartes, *Discourse on Method*, p. 11.

23. Leibniz, *Die Philosophischen Schriften*, ed. Gerhardt (1890; rpt. Hildesheim: Georg Olms Verlagbuchhandlung, 1961), VII, 157.

24. Perelman, *Le Champ de l'argumentation*, p. 278.

25. I.A. Richards, *The Philosophy of Rhetoric* (New York: Oxford University Press, 1936), p. 16.

26. A. Henry, "La reviviscense des métaphores," *Métonymie et métaphore* (Paris: C. Klincksieck, 1971), pp. 143-153.

27. Pascal, *Pensées*, 181.

28. Gaston Bachelard, *Le Rationalisme appliqué* (Paris: Presses Universitaires de France, 1949), p. 22. See *The New Rhetoric*, p. 406.

29. Stephen C. Pepper, *World Hypotheses* (Berkeley: University of California Press, 1942).

30. Dorothy Emmet, *The Nature of Metaphysical Thinking* (London: Macmillan & Co., 1945).

31. *Review of Metaphysics* 16 (1962-1963), 237-258, 450-472, at 472.

32. H. Blumenberg, *Paradigmen zu einer Metaphorologie* (Bonn: 1962).

33. Jacques Derrida, "White Mythology: Metaphor in the Text of Philosophy," trans. F.C.T. Moore, *New Literary History* 6 (1974), 5-74. See also Derrida, "La mythologie blanche," *Poétique* 2 (1971), 1-52.

34. Paul Ricoeur, *The Rule of Metaphor*, pp. 259-272.

11. The Dissociation of Ideas

1. *Critique of Pure Reason*, pp. 409-415.

2. *The New Rhetoric*, pp. 416-417.

3. *Phaedrus* 247d-248b.

4. *The New Rhetoric*, p. 421.

5. Ibid., p. 420.

6. Bergson, *Creative Evolution*, trans. Arthur Mitchell (New York: H. Holt, 1911), p. 302.

7. Sartre, *Being and Nothingness*, pp. xliv-xlvi. See *The New Rhetoric*, p. 419.

8. Martin Buber, *I and Thou* (New York: Charles Scribner & Sons, 1958), pp. 38-39, 60-61. See *The New Rhetoric*, p. 436.

9. Jacques Maritain, *The Range of Reason* (New York: Charles Scribner's Sons, 1952), p. 83.

10. Sartre, *Being and Nothingness*, p. 137.

11. Edmund Husserl, *The Crisis of European Sciences and Transcendental Phenomenology*, trans. David Carr (Evanston: Northwestern University Press, 1970), p. 15. "The genuine spiritual struggles of European humanity as such take the form of

struggles between philosophies—or nonphilosophies, which retain the word but not the task—and the actual and still vital philosophies."

12. *The New Rhetoric,* pp. 436-442.

13. Nelly Cormeau, *L'Art de François Mauriac,* (Paris: Grosset, 1951), pp. 183-84.

14. "Welche Religion ich bekenne? Kein von allen!/ Die du mir nennst.—Und warum Keine?—Aus Religion!" See *The New Rhetoric,* p. 442. See also Perelman, "Perspectives rhétoriques sur les problèmes sémantiques," *Logique et analyses,* 1974, p. 244; English version in *The New Rhetoric and the Humanities,* pp. 82-90.

15. Cocteau, "Plain-Chant," *Empreintes,* May-July, 1950, p. 9.

16. *The New Rhetoric,* p. 444.

17. Ibid., pp. 217-218.

18. Pascal, *Pensées,* 686.

19. Charles Leslie Stevenson, "Persuasive Definitions," *Mind* 27 (1938), pp. 331-350.

20. Ch. Perelman, "Une conception de la philosophie," *Revue de l'Institut de Sociologie* (Brussels, 1940), pp. 11-12.

21. Spinoza, *Ethics,* trans. R.H.M. Elwes (New York: Dover, 1951), Part III, "Definitions of the Emotions," pp. 173-184.

22. Berkeley, *Three Dialogues Between Hylas and Philonous,* Third Dialogue, in *The Works of George Berkeley,* Vol. II, p. 261.

23. Jean Paulhan, *Les fleurs de Tarbes, ou, La Terreur dans les lettres* (Paris: Gallimard, 1941).

12. Fullness of Argumentation and Strength of Arguments

1. "Pragmatic Arguments," in Ch. Perelman, *The Idea of Justice and the Problem of Argument,* pp. 196-207.

2. Bossuet, *Sermons,* Vol. II, pp. 690-91. See *The New Rhetoric,* p. 469.

3. "Logique et Rhétorique," in Perelman and Olbrechts-Tyteca, *Rhétorique et Philosophie* (Paris: Presses Universitaires de France, 1952), p. 20.

4. See *The New Rhetoric,* p. 471.

5. Demosthenes *On the Crown* 3.
6. Quintilian *Institutio oratoria*, 6. 3. 74. See *The New Rhetoric*, p. 489.

13. The Order of Arguments in a Discourse

1. *Rhetoric* 1414a-b.
2. *Rhetoric* 1415a, 25-34.
3. Cicero *Partitiones oratoriae* 46.
4. Pierre de la Ramée, *Dialectique*, p. 145.
5. *Discourse on Method*, p. 42.
6. Ibid., p. 50.
7. Ibid.
8. Ibid., p. 62.
9. Ibid., p. 53.
10. Plato *Phaedrus* (trans. Jowett) 264c.

14. The Realm of Rhetoric

1. Plato *Phaedrus* 273.
2. Plato *Gorgias* 518.
3. Aristotle *Nicomachean Ethics* 1094b. 23-25.
4. Aristotle *Rhetoric* 1391b. 7-21.
5. H. Gouhier, "La résistance au vrai et le problème cartésien d'une philosophie sans rhétorique," *Retorico e Barocco*, ed. E. Castelli (Rome: Fratelli Bocca,1955), pp. 85-97.
6. *Meditations*, p. 17.
7. Ibid., p. 35.
8. Ibid., p. 51.
9. *Discourse on Method*, p. 14.
10. Ibid., p. 15.
11. G. Frey, "Die Logik als Empirische Wissenschaft," *La Théorie de l'argumentation* (Louvain: Nauwelaerts, 1963), pp. 240-262.
12. P. Lorenzen, "Methodisches Denken," ibid., pp. 219-232. See also Lorenzen, *Einführung in die operative Logik* (Berlin:

Springer, 1955), and *Formal Logic*, trans. Frederick J. Crosson (Dordrecht: D. Reidel, 1965).

13. Karl R. Popper, *The Logic of Scientific Discovery* (New York: Basic Books, 1961).

14. Ch. Perelman, "Self-Evidence and Proof," *The Idea of Justice and the Problem of Argument*, pp. 109-125. Also, "De l'évidence en métaphysique," *Le Champ de l'argumentation*, pp. 236-248.

15. Plato *Euthyphro* 7.

16. Ch. Perelman, *Logique juridique*, Par. 37, 40, 48. 97.

17. Ch. Perelman, *Justice*, p. 87, and "What the Philosopher May Learn from the Study of Law," Appendix to *Justice*, p. 110.

18. M. Genett, "La rhétorique restreinte," *Communications*, 16, 1970, p. 158.

19. Walter Jens, *Von Deutscher Rede* (Munich: Piper, 1969), p. 45.

20. V. Florescu, *La retorica nel suo sviluppo storico* (Bologna: Il Mulino, 1971), and Ch. Perelman, "The New Rhetoric, A Theory of Practical Reasoning," *Great Ideas Today* pp. 272-312.

Index